NEVER BUY
ANOTHER STOCK AGAIN

NEVER BUY
ANOTHER STOCK AGAIN

*The Investing Portfolio that Will
Preserve Your Wealth and Your Sanity*

DAVID GAFFEN

Vice President, Publisher: Tim Moore
Associate Publisher and Director of Marketing: Amy Neidlinger
Executive Editor: Jeanne Glasser
Editorial Assistant: Myesha Graham
Operations Manager: Gina Kanouse
Senior Marketing Manager: Julie Phifer
Publicity Manager: Laura Czaja
Assistant Marketing Manager: Megan Colvin
Cover Designer: Chuti Prasertsith
Managing Editor: Kristy Hart
Project Editors: Jovana San Nicolas-Shirley and Kelly Craig
Copy Editor: Geneil Breeze
Proofreader: Williams Woods Publishing Services
Indexer: WordWise Publishing Services
Senior Compositor: Gloria Schurick
Manufacturing Buyer: Dan Uhrig

© 2011 by Pearson Education, Inc.
Publishing as FT Press
Upper Saddle River, New Jersey 07458

FT Press offers excellent discounts on this book when ordered in quantity for bulk purchases or special sales. For more information, please contact U.S. Corporate and Government Sales, 1-800-382-3419, corpsales@pearsontechgroup.com. For sales outside the U.S., please contact International Sales at international@pearson.com.

Company and product names mentioned herein are the trademarks or registered trademarks of their respective owners.

Printed in the United States of America

First Printing December 2010

ISBN-10: 0-13-707155-8
ISBN-13: 978-0-13-707155-5

Pearson Education LTD.
Pearson Education Australia PTY, Limited.
Pearson Education Singapore, Pte. Ltd.
Pearson Education Asia, Ltd.
Pearson Education Canada, Ltd.
Pearson Educación de Mexico, S.A. de C.V.
Pearson Education—Japan
Pearson Education Malaysia, Pte. Ltd.

Library of Congress Cataloging-in-Publication Data

Gaffen, David Aaron, 1973-

  Never buy another stock again : the investing portfolio that will preserve your wealth and your sanity / David Gaffen. — 1st ed.

    p. cm.

  ISBN 978-0-13-707155-5 (hardback : alk. paper) 1. Investments. 2. Index mutual funds. I. Title.

  HG4521.G17 2010

  332.6—dc22

                                        2010024184

For my children, Lily and Noah.

Contents

Acknowledgments

The entirety of this book would not be possible without the counsel and experience of my agent, Jeffrey Krames, who contacted me about writing a book more than two years ago and before I had any idea as to what I might want to write about. Needless to say, he was hands-on as ideas were developed and has been a great ally. The book would not exist without him.

I need to thank, as well, my editor, Jeanne Glasser, who has been steady in her belief in the book's value, provided careful and useful edits, and was encouraging and understanding through the entire process. Jeanne and the rest of the editing and production staff at FT Press are crucial to this book's success.

I cannot go without the acknowledgement of those in the industry who provided wise thoughts and took the time to explain their views extensively about this market. I interviewed many during the course of this book's development, but in particular would like to mention Jeffrey Rubin of Birinyi Associates, Diane Garnick of Invesco, and Rob Arnott of Research Affiliates, who deepened my understanding of the markets.

I would also like to mention the journalists who have inspired me over the years and contributed to my growth as a writer and reporter, including but not limited to Suzanne Pavkovic, David Mark, Sailaja Sastry, Todd Bell, Dan Carroll, Jamie Heller, Aaron Task, John Edwards, Ron Lieber, David Geracioti, Matt Barthel, Geoffrey Lewis, Pat Fitzgibbons, Mark Gongloff, Cindy Perman, Tim Annett, Jennifer Ablan, Bill Schomberg, and Chris Sanders. I owe a massive debt to fellow traveler Erin Arvedlund, who prodded me throughout the process and provided valuable tips to make this book much better than it could have been without her efforts.

My thanks also go to my employer, Thomson Reuters, which gave me the support and time to take on this project. This work does not reflect the opinions of my employer as it is solely my effort.

I'd be nowhere without my mother and father, and my sister, Jessica, who remember the days when I'd struggle through English class due to a lack of interest in writing. How things change.

This book came about at a rather busy period in my life, coming a few months before and after the birth of my second child, Noah. In between late-night feedings I set these words to paper, often sitting on a stepstool with my laptop propped up on the bed while my daughter, Lily, was across the hall trying to sleep. My children are my treasure, and the need to comfort my daughter by being in her vicinity was an interesting way for me to discipline myself by using the time spent upstairs to write more.

I'm going to end with some words for my wife, Dana, who has been unwavering in her support for me. It's not easy to juggle two kids and full-time jobs, but she was there to pick me up when I was feeling frustrated and celebrate the high points with me as well. This book is for you. I love you very much.

About the Author

David Gaffen has been covering the ups-and-downs of the financial markets for 15 years. He is currently an editor at Reuters, overseeing a team that reports on the stocks, bonds and foreign exchange markets. He was the founding writer and editor of the *Wall Street Journal's* MarketBeat blog, which he wrote for more than three years, and was nominated for an Editor and Publisher Eppy Award. He has made numerous TV and radio appearances, including Fox Business, CNN International, and NPR. He lives in Westchester County, New York, with his wife and two children.

While this book was written during his tenure as a Reuters editor, Reuters has not been involved with the content or tone of this book, which are his responsibility alone.

Introduction

I come from a family of careful investors. There's a theory that people who have not experienced the kind of hardships that Americans faced throughout the Great Depression are more cavalier with their money, but that didn't extend to my family. At the end of every month, I take my spare change, put it into paper coin rolls, and deposit them at the bank, a habit learned from my grandfather. He was one of the all-time great penny-pinchers, who did suffer through the Depression.

But many in recent years forgot about the past—and they repeated it in horrific fashion. Investors with little or no experience in markets were lured into investing in stocks after more than two decades of terrific gains in the equity market, and they got their head handed to them after tech stocks tanked in the early part of the 2000s and the rest of the market was destroyed in the last part of the decade. Stocks have since come back dramatically and then faltered again, leaving many investors wondering just what to do and whether they'd do better just to leave their money under the mattress.

I didn't write this book to validate your feelings of fear. I've been watching and investing in markets for 15 years as a financial reporter and editor. I think I've learned a few things, but much of what I've learned hasn't been emphasized by big brokerages or popular media.

I originated, and for three years was the primary writer of, the *Wall Street Journal's* MarketBeat blog, one of the most popular blogs on WSJ.com's Web site. Now I work as an editor at the newswire Reuters overseeing the markets group, so I have a close eye on the ups and downs of the volatile stock market. I've come to understand that most investors don't adequately understand the risks embedded in the stock market, and I'm here to try to explain some of them. In the years I've been writing about markets during my years at TheStreet.com, the *Wall Street Journal*, and now Reuters, I've met many investors who thought they had it all figured out, and I've also known many who understood the market was an unforgiving beast that could move against them at any time. Those who kept their guard up did better.

In reality, much of the best advice doesn't stray far from my grandfather's desk in his basement, where I watched him as he hunched over, meticulously putting quarters into rolls.

As someone who has been monitoring the markets for the better part of 15 years, I can say for sure that stocks are not the best—and sometimes one of the worst asset classes, because there are times when the stock market, when taking out transaction costs, management fees, and inflation, really does not give you much at all. But this book is not about finding some kind of new way to avoid the asset class that has been the mainstay of investing for decades, because stocks have provided strong returns overall that other investments, like bonds, cannot match.

This book has another purpose: To let you know you don't have to bother with individual stocks at all. Those investors who aren't willing, or do not have the time, to adequately research individual stocks in the equity market should start instead with index funds. Stocks can't be ignored completely, and to stick your head in the sand and pretend you're going to fund your retirement with bonds and not much else would be just as foolish as relentlessly buying equities no matter how bad the selloff.

Along with that, this book will show how a little bit of flexibility and common sense can go a long way to preserving your assets. And keeping your itchy fingers away from the keyboard will help prevent you from ruining your returns with excessive trading while increasing your anxiety. Because if trading costs and management fees are going to kill your returns, it makes the most sense that you should try to cut those down to as little as possible. Thankfully, there are ways to do this.

I'm going to focus on getting you to put much of your investing assets into index-style investments and exchange-traded funds that track major indexes. You're going to have to limit your trading and avoid high-cost brokerages to keep your costs low, and you're going to learn the importance of rebalancing your portfolio to help keep you on the path you want to be on for retirement. Finally, there's diversification, but this diversification is much broader than what you're accustomed to hearing about.

The main practical suggestions for you are in Chapter 10, "Putting It All Together," where I break down my ideal portfolio, one that's less equity-centric and designed to keep costs low. Before that, I'm going to look at ways investors get themselves into trouble and how you can avoid perilous situations—and also how to understand that they can't be circumvented completely.

1

Starting Over

"Managing money is difficult, time-consuming, draining, and a totally alien experience for almost everyone who has come out of the educational system of the United States, where, if you are lucky, you may have learned the difference between a stock and a bond."

Jim Cramer, *Jim Cramer's Real Money: Sane Investing in an Insane World*, 2005

Visitors to this planet from another galaxy in the late 1990s or through most of the last decade would have probably bet the national pastime was not baseball, football, or any other sport, or even reality television—but the stock market. Investing has long since ceased to be the boring activity your grandparents and parents engaged in (usually by purchasing safe securities like zero-coupon bonds) and a run-and-gun activity full of amusement for people willing to sit in front of the computer screen for hours at a time—and there are many such people.

That's because the 1996-2007 period featured two of the greatest bull market runs the U.S. market has ever seen, each of which carried stocks beyond most expectations—from 1996 to 2000 and the 2003-2007 market. With that came the ballooning of incredible expectations on the part of investors. The prowess of the market extended beyond its initial purpose of growing one's assets, but instead the investor class had come to believe that virtually all of the nation's problems could be solved through the wonders of financial markets.

Unlike the post-Depression era, when mom-and-pop investors shunned stocks, investors in this era were conditioned to believe that stocks would always rebound after any and every kind of decline, no matter how precipitous.

This begets a serious misunderstanding of the reality of the risk in the equity market. The prevailing wisdom—that you could never lose money on stocks in the long run—coalesced into a few investing tenets that took over the psyche of the traditional investor. Think of the following three rules as the investor's mantra during this time:

1. Buying and holding stocks is the only strategy.

2. When stocks fall, buy more stocks. Selling is for losers.

3. When confused, see rules #1 and #2.

Essentially, investors were instructed to buy, regardless of the economic situation or short-term fluctuations, because invariably, stocks would rebound. These precipitous drops were merely a buying opportunity (regardless of how much of one's capital was tied up in these supposedly amazing investments that had recently given up substantial value).

This type of learned behavior, which relies on a modicum of historical knowledge and a bit of hope, is difficult to change. Just as the post-Depression era investors missed out on substantial gains in markets because of ingrained prejudice against riskier investments, the reverse was the case with investors of this generation, conditioned to see every pullback as just another reason to keep hungrily buying stocks. Investing, generally thought of as a staid activity, captured the cultural zeitgeist.

In late 1996, Alan Greenspan, in testifying to Congress, used a phrase to describe the state of affairs regarding the financial markets that, for his remaining years as Federal Reserve chairman, would forever be associated with him, asking whether "irrational exuberance" had "unduly escalated asset values." His pessimistic "irrational exuberance" phrasing prompted a sell-off on Wall Street that day, and garnered him scathing criticism from just about everyone.

More than a decade and two harsh recessions later, it's clear the chairman was onto something—even though he had stepped back from those remarks later, by arguing that asset bubbles could not be identified, and therefore the Fed, the authority in charge of keeping interest rates at proper levels, could not do anything about it.

In those years investors enjoyed the fruits of easy credit and technological breakthroughs that caused stocks to skyrocket to new levels. This culminated with the ascent of the Dow Jones Industrial Average to top 14,000 in October 2007. (At the time of Greenspan's speech, the Dow was marking time at about 6,400.) And in that time, the Fed chairman became something of a minor celebrity himself, inspiring a "Get Exuberant!" fan Web site and being lauded with the moniker of "Maestro" for his seemingly impervious ability to navigate markets through troubled waters.

Oddly enough, between 1996 and June 2009, while stocks had put together a healthy 53 percent on a total return basis since Greenspan's ill-received remarks in 1996, it was dwarfed by another asset—a bit less risky one, the risk-free, three-month Treasury bill! An investor who bought treasury bills in 1996 and consistently reinvested them would, by the end of June 2009, have racked up a 56 percent return, according to Bespoke Investment Group, a research firm in Harrison, New York. That's about three percentage points better for an investment that couldn't be safer or more uncomplicated. And that 53 percent gain in stocks only came if one never pulled out of the market and then later picked a bad moment to put money back into stocks. Mis-timing the market is one of the hallmarks of the individual investor, and it's one that served them particularly poorly in the last 13 years. (Note: The subsequent outperformance of stocks in late 2009 and the first half of 2010 left the three-month bill in the dust, but it shouldn't really even be a race in the first place.)

During that period, a cottage industry of market mavens sprouted up. That's not surprising: After all, in 1983, just 19 percent of Americans owned stocks, most of those being direct investments in companies by the very wealthy. By 1998, that figure increased to about 63 percent (counting mutual funds and retirement accounts), and it was up to about 68 percent in 2007, though again, most of the growth has come from ownership of mutual funds and in retirement accounts.[1]

Through that period, the frequent refrain from investors, particularly those with only a cursory knowledge of equities, was that stocks were the best investment, bar none, and investors had to hold them ad infinitum. In doing so, you'd not only be helping yourself, you'd be doing a patriotic thing by buying into the great U.S. capital system, and you'd also be sure to have a great time as well.

Enough

The term "catharsis" is an ancient Greek word that means "purification" or "cleansing." It's that moment when a group of individuals, having finally exhausted their patience, reaches an emotional peak and collectively cries, "Enough!" For a time, it appeared that the 2000-2002 period, which featured the demise of the technology bubble, might serve as this moment for scores of investors. It was not, though, thanks to low interest rates that spurred a frenzy of borrowing—money that was put into the stock market.

The 2008 period seems more likely to serve as catharsis. The horrific debacle in the financial markets revealed a financial structure built on the shifting sands of borrowed money and assets that could not be valued. The likelihood is that the stock market has seen its best days for some time.

But the market's 2009-2010 rally suggests that old habits die hard. So this book is intended in part as catharsis—to jar you out of the thinking that has permeated the mind of the individual investor, mostly through osmosis and the droning of the litany of pundits on television mostly arguing the same thing: That you should leave your money alone and not worry, because in the end, it'll all work out. Does such advice make sense in any other aspect of life? Nobody expects automobiles to run in perpetuity without tune-ups and oil changes; houses that go without upkeep aren't so pretty when the grass is over-grown and the paint is peeling. But a portfolio of investments, some-how, should be set aside in the expectation that you can wake up, Rip Van Winkle-style, some three or four decades later with your retire-ment goals achieved and your worries cast away in the wind.

It doesn't work that way. That said, others like to take things to the other extreme. Financial television features a daily assault of com-mercials designed to convince you that your investments are some-how missing something without this new product, preferably one you can trade often. It's not the same thing as the relentless pumping of the new investments that cropped up during the technology bubble, but it is faddish in its approach, and in a way involves investment in the next hot money-maker.

In this book I suggest avoiding all that and instead advise concen-trating on preservation of capital and realistic expectations. Most peo-ple say their expectations are modest: They expect returns of 8 to 10 percent each year. But a few years of outperformance, such as what existed in the late 1990s and middle part of this decade, has a way of upping one's need for greed. People become less satisfied with mod-est outcomes, particularly if they see others doing better.

The main point of this book is that most people should avoid buy-ing individual stocks. It is a lot harder than it looks. The majority of small investors simply do not have the time or emotional make-up to pick individual stocks. A much better alternative is stock index funds or exchange-traded funds (ETFs). Not only are they cheaper, but you are much more likely to walk away having made money.

Investing is not like Wii Tennis or Sudoku: It's not a game. The decisions you make affect you for the rest of your life. A few people in the world have enough money to throw it around on every fad that comes up, but more than likely, they didn't get rich that way. Investing for one's later years or education for children cannot be done over if it doesn't work out the first time, which is why it is important to be prudent. It's why it is important not to allow hackneyed clichés to take the place of sound understanding of one's goals, how to achieve those goals, and avoid deviating from them just for a chance to play in what the popular media portray as a quizzical game where everyone wins. It's time to say, enough.

Deprogramming

Part of what caused this amazing run in the equity market was an unprecedented period of relatively stable economic growth. After the harsh recession of the early 1980s, the economy suffered just one contraction between 1982 and 2001, in the early 1990s. Fed chairman Greenspan sometimes talked of the "Great Moderation," the period of time when economic cycles became less volatile and less disruptive, and certainly this period, encompassing nearly two decades, qualifies.

During this period, several significant developments occurred that facilitated the greater involvement of investors in the equity market. For one, interest rates declined from double-digit rates as part of Fed chairman Paul Volcker's effort to choke off inflation. Lower rates supported borrowing, which supported the equity market.

Second, the creation of the 401(k) plan, the 403(b) retirement vehicle, along with the individual retirement account and specifically designed accounts for individuals to sock money away for education for children, piqued interest in equity investments. "There were all of these plans to save for retirement that hadn't been there before, and suddenly America had a way to invest in the stock market in a tax advantaged way," said Kevin Flynn, head of Avalon Asset Management, an investment advisory in Massachusetts. "There was a wonderful excitement in the investment world for years."[2]

The spirit of this feeling was captured in a commercial for discount brokerage Charles Schwab in the late 1990s. Olympic skier Picabo Street is shown in a weight room talking about an unspecified "crash." Since she had broken her leg in an awful wipe-out the year before, the natural assumption was that she was discussing skiing. She then makes it clear that she isn't speaking about skiing at all—she's referencing the one-day, 22 percent decline in stocks in 1987, which she concludes was a buying opportunity, and not a crash.

With that in mind, the massive explosion in interest in the stock market rewarded investors with staggering outperformance. The Dow industrials put together a streak of nine consecutive years of positive returns, and between 1996 and 1999, the Dow industrials returned more than 22 percent in four of five years (the straggler was a still-terrific 16 percent gain in 1998). It's no wonder that the three-year bear market lasting from 2000 to 2002 did not dissuade investors from the by-now accepted behavior that buying again was the most prudent course of action.

The hangover from those gains was easy for investors to dismiss. Plenty of people simply brushed off those losses, rationalizing the 2000-2002 period as a consequence of overly optimistic buying of Internet companies that did not make money. (The 9/11 attacks also hastened the decline in equities.) Investors went back to their old ways, buying heavily in stocks—and as we shall see, real estate—but this time, doing it by borrowing lots of money, using their houses as a casino with home equity loans. And what was merely risky—putting all of one's eggs in one basket, that basket being the stock market—became downright foolish when they were somebody else's eggs.

It's been a tough lesson to learn. Since 2003 investors have found that the old saw about stocks being the best investment for long periods of time has not held up. Since 2000, the Dow has finished higher in four years, and finished lower in five years, including the devastating 34 percent decline in 2008.

But even after such a lackluster period of performance—what is already being referred to as America's "lost decade" in equities—learned behavior is hard to change. There's an odd paradox at work here: Investors are told to avoid selling stocks in response to a sharp decline, because that's considered "panicking." But frenzied upward moves in equities are not met with the same cautious advice—investors are instead told they'd better act lest they "miss the rally." Either way the prevailing advice defaults in favor of buying more stocks, and also happens to be the one guaranteed to cause the average investor the most stress—you're either sweating out sharp declines in stocks while doing nothing, or instructed to dive right in again after losing lots of dough. This is a particularly curious set of rules to follow, because long-run statistics show that most major markets, at one time or another in their history, have lost about 75 percent of their value. This tends to happen when the greatest number of people have convinced themselves of the market's value and are most leveraged to continued success in the market.

Even after the horrific bear market that commenced in late 2007 and saw stocks fall to 12-year lows in March 2009, investor behavior has still been slow to change. Between March 2009 and late August 2009, the stock market rallied by 50 percent, and the investor populace, forever convinced of the stock market's superiority, rushed headlong back into the equity market. In January 2009, assets in money market funds, a safe, cashlike investment, hit a peak at $3.92 trillion. By the end of August, more than $300 billion in that capital shifted out of those money market funds and back into stocks, according to Mizuho Securities.[3]

Confidence among investors, while not shattered, has been eroded. After the sharp move back into the market among mom-and-pop investors in the summer of 2009, money market fund assets remained at a stable level as the market continued to rally, suggesting investors had become a bit more gun-shy, and equity inflows, according to the Investment Company Institute, trailed inflows into fixed income funds, suggesting that the overall appetite for risk has shifted away from stocks. But it's hard to say whether hope springs eternal here—in 2010, data on flows into equity funds started to show, once again, that investors were getting back into stocks, after a gain of more than 60 percent, the biggest 12-month rally in the history of the Standard & Poor's 500 stock index. Once again, individuals are showing their shortcomings, and they appear, once again, all-too-willing to forgive and forget, and go back to what's familiar. Are you one of those investors? Did you stay away for 2009 and then jump back into the market in 2010 after a spectacular rally that had already concluded? You're not alone—and your sudden enthusiasm comes just as institutions, which have made hay off the 2009 gains, are finding the environment a little more circumspect.

Investor tolerance for risk has been at least somewhat altered, though—a report from consultancy Spectrem Group published in October 2009 noted that newly conservative investors with assets of $100,000 to $1 million were unlikely to change those behaviors in the long term, citing the sharp decline in their portfolios. Cash had become king, and bond market investments looked better as well. They were also monitoring their investments more closely, as 55 percent of the nearly 2,000 surveyed said their losses had "seriously impacted" their long-term financial plans.[4]

The greater attention to detail is a positive development, as is a newfound realization that the market would not provide rich gains for year after year. In a sense, this is the new version of the Great Moderation—the moderation in investment behavior that deals with the reality of gyrations in financial assets and attempts to insulate against it, rather than simply assuming all goes for the best. Time will tell, however, whether this recent streak of cautiousness we've all adopted goes by the wayside if stocks continue to perform well, or whether behavior has been changed irrevocably. The way things usually go is that people swing from one extreme to another—the average American remained deathly afraid of the stock market for years after the

Great Depression. Once the love affair with equities was rekindled in the mid-1980s, though, it was impossible to give up for so many. Margin borrowing rose, people borrowed on home equity to finance purchases in the stock market, and America made unlikely celebrities of Fed chairman Alan Greenspan, CNBC anchor Maria Bartiromo, and Jim Cramer of TheStreet.com.

Now, after an ugly two-year recession that has left the economy overleveraged and on shaky footing, Wall Street doesn't have a lot of friends. Data on mutual fund inflows suggests that the ingrained mistrust of brokerages, which remained at a simmer when things were going well, is red hot. You're looking to preserve your capital, and right now the government seems like a better place than anywhere else.

But that would be a fool-hardy approach, because the government bond market is likely to provide very limited returns.

We'll get to the specifics of what to do there in a bit. The first task, however, is deprogramming: It's retraining your mind to understand that the reflexive advice you've been hearing for the last decade-and-a-half (in the face of all evidence pointing the other direction) should be largely ignored. There are a number of good lessons in the long-run historic data in the stock market, which we'll look at shortly, but few seem to acknowledge that simply repeating mantras about staying in the market at all times is not the path to success. Mutual fund data, for now, seems to suggest that investors may have finally gotten the idea when it comes to this—and it only took a couple of really, really hard blows to the head to figure it out. If the definition of insanity is doing the same thing time and again while expecting a different result, well, the bulk of stock pundits would have been put in a white room with padded walls a long time ago.

Those of you looking for easy answers will not find any such comfort here, and you should be wary of anyone who gives you the impression that this—managing your money—is an easy task. It is not. It will frequently be stressful, and it is naturally going to be emotionally taxing at times. Yes, it can be fun—particularly when things are going well. But they're not going to always go well. And the complex nature of it is part of the reason why I am advising, in general, to avoid complicating already tough decisions with individual stock investments. Your time is better spent elsewhere. In these pages we will go through the various basics for getting your portfolio set up, so your assets can be in sound shape for what is likely to be several more years of tumult.

But the first lessons are going to be in psychology and in nerves. Those who stay alert and skeptical tend to fare better, even if for a few years they were considered stodgy because they refused to go all-in and bet on the most aggressive investment that was being proffered by talking heads and Wall Street brokerages. I've also been investing for years—making plenty of mistakes along the way—and have come to realize that those who don't have the time to try to outperform markets should look to work with their money as best as they can through keeping their costs low and their losses at a minimum. It's simple advice, as much of the advice in this market tends to be, but it's not well-followed, as the historic performance of the individual will show you. Learning that there are limitations does not mean you can't put together a portfolio that will stay relatively strong during tough periods—you have to accept some losses, after all—and do well during the good times.

With that, it's time for a few aphorisms that could come from the mind of Al Franken's Stuart Smalley character from "Saturday Night Live," the relentlessly optimistic self-help counselor. Consider them ways to keep yourself humble and in a cautious frame of mind when the market gets out of control. Here are Gaffen's four rules for investing:

1. You don't know everything. This is okay.

2. You're not missing something by not buying _____.

3. It's okay to move money from one asset to another.

4. It's okay if you lose money. Accept this as part of investing.

Much of the conventional wisdom the market belches out revolves either around the notion that you can do this better than anyone, so go for it!, or that you should give your money to someone who presumably does know everything. It's the nature of this market that we will continue to strive for that ideal, that market-beating mechanism that will work for infinity, and not just a lucky streak of six years or something, which we'll talk about at length in the coming pages. But admitting you don't have all of the information is merely prudent. Recognizing your own limitations as an investor is crucial; it's one reason why you picked up this book! This will also allow you to keep your objectives clear and your philosophy simple: that low-cost investments, keeping yourself away from big losses in your portfolio, taking advantage of opportunities that will keep taxes low, and strategic shifting of your money and proper diversification, should keep you in reasonably solid shape for the bulk of your investing life.

The second point—that you're not missing something by skipping on the fad of the week—is key. It's one we'll discuss at great length, as many people have convinced themselves of the better mousetrap, only to lose everything. This is fine if you have a million dollars lying around to play with. (I still don't recommend it, but knock yourself out.) But your nest egg is not for playtime. If the industry or stock in question becomes successful, buying large, total market indexes will eventually see the fruits of this, and if it doesn't, well, you haven't lost much. This goes for new products or different asset classes that somehow are advertised as insurance against any and all pitfalls (Gold! Commodities! Hedge funds! Alternative Assets!). But with the exception of a government debt instrument that's rolled over consistently from now until you eventually die and leave your assets to your children, there are almost no guarantees in terms of getting your money back. Annuities have such guarantees, true, but there are costs to be considered as well. Pensions have a defined guarantee, although with so many big municipalities and states in trouble around the U.S., who knows how that'll turn out. But for self-directed investments, other than government debt, the guarantees are few. And government debt is not going to get you the kind of asset appreciation that will fund your retirement, not if you live for 30 years after you finally turn in your keys at the office for the last time. This is the reason why other riskier assets are the ones people lean on in their portfolios.

The third point—that it's okay to move money around—is one that's been lost for decades amid the ridiculous rise in the equity market. It took mutual fund investors a while after the gut-wrenching losses of 2008 and early 2009, but mutual fund data shows investors getting back to the stock market in 2010—after they'd already missed what is likely to be the best rally of their lifetime. And it's a sign of the reflexive belief in the stock market's role as savior of all that is good and holy. But you're allowed to sell your equity holdings if they are moving against you; simply leaving them alone does not make you prudent or heroic. With the proliferation of exchange-traded funds and mutual funds that invest in currencies, commodities, real estate, corporate debt, and hard assets, you're not forced to stick with a mundane stocks/bonds split.

The last point is perhaps the most important. Many people open individual retirement accounts and 401(k) accounts and overweight in stocks, particularly if there are hot funds available looking to capture strong performance in bank stocks, small-caps, technology, emerging markets, or corporate debt. But suddenly, things aren't going well, and now that fund in question is down substantially from where you purchased it. Well, the historical data is not going to help you. The fund is up 30 percent in the last two years? That's great, but for someone else—you weren't there for it. So take a deep breath and repeat after me: I'm allowed to sell this. You've got a lousy fund that's not getting anywhere? I'm not talking about a fund that's only up a few percentage points while everything else runs to the moon—that's perfectly acceptable. I'm talking about a dog, something that's getting killed, down

15 percent while the rest of your assets go nowhere. If it worries you that much, get rid of it—you've lost 15 percent on it but you won't lose any more.

If you do sell certain investments, you're going to risk the possibility that they come back in a big way. This has to be accepted. You're going to risk also that cash does nothing (as it tends to do). But small losses help you prevent big losses. Funds can be repurchased, and if you're so enamored of this one investment, keep it on your radar screen and perhaps get it back later when it has stabilized. Everyone makes mistakes when they invest—I left my money in the stock market much longer than I should have amid the meltdown in 2008—but keeping those mistakes small will preserve your capital.

First, though, we have to start with the deprogramming. In the 1960s Timothy Leary exhorted a generation to "Turn On, Tune In, Drop Out." I'm not suggesting anything so drastic as to remove yourself from the market entirely. But there's a lot of noise that can be filtered from your daily diet, and it starts with most forms of media, but particularly the television. So we're going to drop out. That means it's time to turn off the racket that is CNBC and the ongoing clamor of upgrades, downgrades, and smugness that makes up the bulk of that station's programming. Most of the station's commentary—other than finance guru Suze Orman—isn't helpful for long-term investment strategy and really only serves to amplify conventional market wisdom and heighten your sense of insecurity. Get shut of it. You need to start with that much. Your retirement does not depend on the next round of corporate earnings or the monthly report on the Federal Reserve's Philadelphia-region business activity index.

From there, it's time to start ignoring the investing blogs that constantly advise shifting from one position to the next, and particularly to leave behind the rumors and stock-touting that make up the bulk of investing discussion boards. This isn't to denigrate blogs: I wrote one for three years covering the ups and downs of the market on a daily basis, and there are many terrific individuals out there watching the market and writing interesting things in the blog format. Many of them, because they're concentrated on one thing, are particularly astute. But consider them the way you consider your favorite sports columnist—something to enjoy without having to follow to the letter.

There are also those (and this is especially true of message boards) that don't go much further than being a tout service. Furthermore, you can go and chuck into the trashcan every magazine telling you about "the best funds to buy now" and can every weekly or daily newspaper yammering on the newest strategy designed to avoid all of the pitfalls that they somehow didn't manage to pick up on when they were advising you to buy the last fad—the one that led the market into the toilet when stocks tanked just a few years ago.

It was this advice that gave birth to the main idea of this book. In a busy daily routine that involves holding down a job, caring for children, maintaining a house, and myriad other responsibilities that many of you have, it's hard to find time for anything. And as a result it requires triage: You have to worry about your money, but the requisite amount of time you need to truly keep track of individual shares is more than a person with a full schedule can bear. You've got to take care of medical expenses, funding your retirement, education for your children, making sure bills are paid, mortgages are taken care of, and taxes are accounted for, in addition to putting your money away in investments that are properly diversified in a number of areas. Within that investment portfolio you have to diversify between stocks, bonds, cash, and a number of other asset classes we'll get at later—and keep track of when it's time to rebalance your portfolio. With all of this in mind, something has to give—and the research into positions on individual shares is a prime candidate, and so are the costs associated with trading and paying for active management that already put you three lengths behind the field before the starting gun has been fired.

Now I know you're probably wondering, is it possible to still put together a portfolio that does well without buying individual stocks?

Most assuredly it is, but it comes from paying attention to your costs, making sure you don't forget about your investments for months on end, and understanding what you need to retire with the kind of life you want. That's plenty of work to do without delving into individual names, particularly when most professionals are already pretty poor at trying to outdo the major market averages in the first place.

And that's another point to consider: There's an argument that simply investing a lot of your money in index funds (which is in part what this book advocates) means you're going to underperform the market no matter what, but I think that's the wrong parameter to begin with. After all, major indexes are representative only of themselves: the Standard & Poor's 500-stock index may rise a certain percentage in a given year and may be averaging 7 or 8 percent per year for the last 30, but if you only need 5 percent a year, the S&P 500 is meaningless. If you need 10 percent, it's just as meaningless—it's only a guide to itself. The goal isn't necessarily going to be to hit the market's average for a number of years, but to garner strong enough returns that will allow you to live as you want in your retirement. If you can do this with nothing but the carried interest from government bonds because you already have a massive nest egg, then good for you—you have little reason to invest in riskier assets. If you're struggling to fund a retirement, the reality is that you're going to have to take more risks. This is all the more reason, however, to keep costs low, so you're spending less of your capital on overhead.

This book is not designed to be defeatist. It's meant to help navigate through tumultuous markets, which we're bound to see more of in the coming years, and also to try to shift away from the reflexive notion that stocks are all that matter when it comes to putting together a portfolio.

Stocks for the Long Run...Or Not

The ascendance of equities as the most important investment in one's portfolio ahead of all else (particularly as many were lobbying to find ways to invest Social Security payments in the stock market) coincided with the underperformance of that very asset class against more conservative investments. An investor who elected, in 1969, to invest in the bond market rather than stocks would have likely outperformed the stock market. According to Chicago-based research firm Ibbotson & Associates, long-term government bonds returned, on average, a compound annualized total return of 8.79 percent since 1969, beating the Standard & Poor's 500-stock index, which gained 8.70 percent in that time. That difference in performance is not dramatic, but it is notable considering the safety of government bonds with the riskier stock market.

What stands out amid the performance of stocks and bonds is that the former remains much more volatile than the latter. Both the bond and stock markets have had great years—the best year for stocks since 1969 was in 1975, when the market rose by 37 percent, and bonds nearly equaled that feat in 1982, gaining 36 percent. On the other hand, a bad year for bonds is 1999, when they fell 6 percent. But stocks are like the proverbial little girl with the little curl in her forehead: When they're good, they're very very good, but when they're bad, they're horrid. In 2008, the S&P fell 37 percent, and many individual names did worse.

Slicing and dicing those figures further brings better results for bonds in some cases, and more favorable outcomes for stocks in others. Government bonds easily beat stocks for the 20-year period beginning in April 1989, returning 9.61 percent, compared with a 7.42 percent gain for the S&P 500. Intermediate-term bond funds (which concentrated on buying bonds that mature in two to seven years) pull in a return of 7.39 percent, just behind the stock index. Stocks do better if the starting point is placed in 1979—a 10.3 percent return compared with a 9.93 percent return for bonds—and of course when the last ten years are considered bonds wipe the floor with the stock market.

The choice between bonds and stocks does tilt in favor of stocks over much longer periods of time. Ibbotson notes that the S&P 500 produced a compound annual average return of 9.44 percent between January 1926 and March 2009, whereas bonds, in that period of time, returned 5.6 percent annually. And Wharton professor Jeremy Siegel used historic data beginning in 1802 to argue for the superiority of equity market returns.

However, those early figures have been challenged by a number of analysts as spotty, relying on just a few stocks to serve as the benchmark for 19th-century figures and overstating the dividend component; others believe the long-run return of stocks is perhaps closer to 7 percent or even 5 percent, as the classic tome *Triumph of the Optimists* points out.

Market mavens hold this kind of history up as a sign that it's folly to consider the bond market as a potentially superior investment. Then again, there are very few people who started investing in 1926 and 83 years later, were still saving for retirement, other than perhaps 900-year-old Jedi master Yoda and Jeanne Calment, the French woman who died in 1997 at the age of 122.

Some would argue that the stock market has not really had a long enough period for one to analyze whether it indeed is truly an outperformer. The S&P 500 has only been around since the 1920s. Historical looks at stocks show that over 200 years, stocks have beaten bonds by about two percentage points, but Rob Arnott, chairman of money manager Research Affiliates, noted to the *Wall Street Journal*[5] that half of that two-point outperformance in stocks comes from the 1949 to 1965 period, when stocks enjoyed a historic run, brought on by the post-war growth period in the U.S.

Notably, this sharp run-up came after nearly two decades of poor performance amid the Great Depression, the original event that turned investors off of equities for decades. Without that post-war period, stocks beat bonds over 200 years by one measly percentage point, and with that one point you get a heck of a lot more volatility and substantial additional risk.

This long-term performance makes investor willingness to place greater hope in the stock market puzzling. Perhaps the desire to invest in stocks comes from the dangling possibilities of riches that an investment in a staid government bond cannot promise. A person buys a bond in the knowledge that he will get his money back, with a steady interest payment. A person buys a stock hoping she's stumbled upon the next Google—which tripled between 2005 and 2007.

Perhaps the psychological preference to stocks comes from the desire for getting the most for as little as possible, or the hope for something bigger and better, which is what equity markets promise. The stock market gets at the very heart of the optimism that is part of human nature. Bonds? Bonds are like eating vegetables.

Investors in stocks are essentially telling the company in question, "Here. Here's my money. Good luck. Hopefully, this will all work out for all of us."

Now, they can point to historical figures, such as steady earnings, past performance of the stock and related companies, or economic growth, for justification of their investment in the unknown. But really, there are only two ways to make money in stocks: Payment of dividends, or later sales of the stock in question at a higher price. These two methods hearken to the two major theories of stock invest-ment—the firm foundation theory and the castle-in-the-sky theory. The former is based on the premise that stocks have an intrinsic value that is a discount on their future earnings and dividends and are val-ued based on that—investing in a stock that is undervalued will pro-duce steady returns over long periods of time. The latter describes the market's psyche of the last two decades, namely that it does not matter what you think of a company's intrinsic value, it only matters that someone else thinks it is worth more. It calls to mind the old saw about two people being chased in the woods by a bear. One of the men expresses doubt that they can outrun the bear, and his friend replies: "I don't have to outrun the bear. I only have to outrun you." Investing since the run-up in the mid-to-late 1990s has been a repeated application of the "greater fool" theory, where one only needs to find another willing investor to buy stuff, another person who cannot outrun the bear.

In the realm of the stock market, many investors employ dividend-seeking strategies, and base their decisions on the companies paying the heftiest dividends back to investors as a percentage of the stock price, which is referred to as the "dividend yield."

For example, say a company priced at $10 a share is paying a $1 dividend per year. When one buys that stock, the investor is guaranteeing themselves at least a 10 percent return—$1 for every $10 spent. If, for instance, the S&P 500's overall dividend yield is about 5 percent, and government bond yields are hovering around 3.5 percent, the decision to buy stocks becomes easier.

But many companies do not pay dividends, and in 2008 and 2009, many have eliminated or curtailed such payments due to the market's problems. (This will reverse in time, though.)

That leaves the second way to make money in stocks—through sales of the shares to someone else. But this relies on expectations that someone else will—based on a company's earnings, cash, assets and other indications—value the company at a higher price than you did. If dividends aren't part of the picture, this is basically a mathematically inclined form of gambling, where an investor hopes someone else will appraise their stock at a higher price than the last person. Yes, many will argue that stocks will appreciate over time based on those expectations for greater growth and steady earnings, and in many cases, this is how it works out. But intrinsically there's still a bet that the other guy is going to look at a particular stock and agree to buy it at a higher price than you did. It depends on an ongoing supply of new investors who believe the investment in question is worth more than the last guy. Don't believe me? Look to James Cramer, the hard-to-miss TV personality who ran (at its peak) the $450 million Cramer Berkowitz hedge fund. In his 2005 book, *Real Money*, Cramer also argued that the stock market had more in common with gambling than almost anything else, even advocating horse-racing guides as a valuable bit of reading for investors.

The argument in favor of buying because of expectations for greater growth is that the economy continues to grow, and companies continue to make more money, which justifies a stock being worth more over the years. And one would think that the traditional measures of valuation—price-to-earnings ratios, earnings growth expectations—would help investors guard against buying stocks when they reach levels that would be considered overvalued. If the market was truly efficient and was able to constantly adjust prices to reflect the true value of an enterprise, this kind of discussion wouldn't need to take place at all.

But in the last several years, the market has become more of a feeding frenzy. On average, investors hold stocks for much shorter periods of time than in the past, as more try to take advantage of buying interest based on unrealistic expectations—which adds to the Ponzi-scheme element of the market. It seems there's no shortage of reasoning (or rationalization, if you prefer) for buying stocks when they reach levels that should nominally be considered too expensive based on history, as long as someone else is buying them.

To say that stocks are a de facto Ponzi scheme is overstating matters—after all, companies that return dividends are giving investors back something for their money, and that dividend comes from earnings. It's not fake. But contrary to the popular disclaimer that "past performance is not a guarantee of future success," most investors rely simply on that. Or as current Credit Suisse strategist Doug Cliggott put it in 1999, "the 'greater fool' theory has been around a long time."[6]

Legions of investors built fortunes (and later lost them) asserting that the Internet would increase productivity, thus obviating all of the old reasons for traditional ways of valuing investments. As a result, the Nasdaq Composite Index, an index heavily concentrated in technology stocks, exploded in the late 1990s. It reached 3000 on November 3, 1999, for the first time, and hit 4000—a 33 percent gain—just two months later. But it wasn't done! The 5000 level was hit in early March.

Convoluted rationalizations led a pair of authors, James K. Glassman and Kevin Hassett, to declare that the popular Dow Jones Industrial Average should reach 36,000 within a few years. This book was published in 1999. This prediction has not turned out so well. Stocks peaked in 2000, and then entered a corrective phase that continues to this day, despite hitting a new high in October 2007. The prediction seemed ridiculous from the outset and has since become the object of scorn, similar to Irving Fisher's assertion in 1929 that stocks had reached a "permanently high plateau."

Those who argue that stocks maintain a superior advantage over equities also can be guilty of looking too closely at U.S. stocks. The world's third largest economy is Japan. That country underwent a boom fueled by excessive speculation in real estate that at one point famously valued the Imperial Palace in Tokyo at more than all of the real estate in California. The country's primary stock market index, the Nikkei, peaked at the end of 1989 at nearly 39,000. Two decades later, the Nikkei trades at about 10,000, or about one-fourth of that market's peak, as the country spent more than a decade trying to pull its banks out of the rubble of the post-boom crisis. Such a situation persists in the United States, where major financial institutions have elected to keep credit tight for fear of more losses.

Bonds, by contrast, are a much more conservative investment, germinating from a more cautious rationale. The investment is a loan, not a prayer. Guarantees of yearly payments are given in return, along with the eventual repayment of the original loan. They're not risk-free, of course: Bonds issued by companies in poor financial shape are more likely to go bankrupt, or default on their debt, and as such merit a higher interest rate. (Government bonds generally do not default, unless they're issued by a government like Argentina or Ecuador, both of whom have reneged on debt payments in recent years.) U.S. government bonds are not in such shape, thanks to your tax dollars.

Not everyone is convinced bonds can continue to outperform the market, noting the unimaginably high inflation of the 1970s and the subsequent decline in those rates as crucial to the bond market's stellar returns of the last four decades. This is unlikely to be repeated, and if it is, it would first require massive rises in bond yields—and therefore, sharp losses in the value of those bonds. "Bond returns were not only much higher than their historical averages, but also higher than their current yields," noted Peng Chen and Roger Ibbotson of Ibbotson and Associates, on Morningstar.com's Web site.[7] They argue that stocks are more likely to outperform in coming years.

The more reductive thinkers in the crowd would look at the steady growth in the bond market and assume that stocks "have to" perform better, in the same way investors expected that the Internet stocks that once reached $150 a share "had to" return to something close to that level. (It's the kind of thinking that assumes a baseball player is "due" to get a hit after going hitless in his previous 14 at-bats—the chances do not change because of previous outcomes.)

Still, those who believe stocks will rebound may yet be right. As we will see, this still does not necessarily mean investors should default to the decades-old recommendation of 60 percent of one's investments in stocks and 40 percent in bonds. It also does not mean investors should try their hand at beating the market through day-trading or active stock market investment.

Stocks indeed can produce strong returns through certain periods of time, and tend to do well after a period of underperformance such as the one that was experienced between 1999 and 2009. But investors can do plenty of damage if they concentrate their funds in all of the wrong stocks, as many found out through the carnage of the past ten years of investing.

Some of you may be looking at this book and thinking a similar thought as many more than likely felt about those tomes that rode the 1999 boom and confidently predicted the market would soar another 30,000 percent in the next week or what have you—that it's just taking advantage of the current bearish trend in stocks, and it's guaranteed to be proven wrong as the market soars in the next few years. But that's not the idea. What I'm trying to do with this book is let people know that:

1. There are options outside of merely accepting that one's money has to be in stocks to gain any kind of real solid return in coming years.

2. It is okay to sell from time to time—not willy-nilly, but you needn't ascribe to some vague notion of putting all of your money away and forgetting about it for 40 years until—voila!— you have enough for retirement.

3. More importantly, it's to allow people to admit that it's okay if they're not adept in buying individual names, that they can ignore "buying on the dips," or "going bargain hunting." It's not a deficit of character to not want to do this. Feeling this way has ruined many a portfolio as you succumb to envy of what the guy next door is doing, as he confidently regales you with tales of his investing prowess. Never mind all that. When the market does badly, he probably does worse.

You can hang in there by limiting your costs and not buying into the game that Wall Street investment houses, brokerages, advertisers, and the popular media has been selling for the last three decades. You can ignore the hype, the carefully constructed ad campaigns that, contrary to what they say, do not make a person feel empowered but make them feel anxious and inadequate for not following the herd. It's true that stock picking is a talent, which we'll demonstrate in coming pages. But it's a talent that most so-called professionals don't even possess, so you needn't feel bad that you don't have it either. What you can do is know where your money is going and make smart decisions but also as few decisions as possible, instead of going down the rabbit hole of constantly trading stocks.

Again, that's not to say that this book has some kind of magic elixir that will beat the market. If that's why you're holding this, I suggest you put it down and go find something else to read. This book is supposed to wake people up.

This book will show how index funds, over long periods of time, can generally get the job done. But this isn't some kind of ode to the joys of indexing, not when holding an index fund over the last decade has been akin to running on a gerbil wheel. This book also looks at how some prominent investors are finding ways to diversify and beat the market with targeted bets on asset classes rather than on sectors, and how a bit of work—through rebalancing, through holdings of bonds, through discipline and understanding emotions—can make you a lot happier in the coming years.

Again, that's not a secret formula. Being in my profession, I know better than to promise the world, or better returns than the next guy's great formula. There are lots of formulas out there; some of them seem to work, and some of them, as I'll demonstrate, are exposed as unworkable.

Going Forward

Over a long period of time it is true that stocks will tend to out-perform the bond market, to say nothing of cash and certain other investments. But that period of time can be so long as to be irrelevant to the greater investing public, which tends to spend about 40 years in prime investing years. Someone who starts to build a nest egg at the age of 25 could have been lucky enough to do so in 1955, withdrawing their funds from equities in the late 1990s to shift to a recommended fixed-income portfolio, and absolutely rocked the long-term averages. But a person who started at age 25 in the mid-1990s got to see tremendous gains before it all went south and has since been treading water for ten years. Some 25-year periods have better annual average returns than others, and yet the person who ended her 25-year invest-ing period with a substantial bear market ended up with less than someone else fortuitous to cap off two-and-a-half decades with a strong bull market.

Shopworn adages should not be construed as investment advice. There are times when buying and holding stocks is the best possible idea, and there are times when buying on pullbacks works like a charm. And there are also instances when both strategies will prove endlessly frustrating.

Not only are individual investors poor at timing the market, there are plenty of professionals that are just as bad. In fact, most of them are pretty bad, and the ones who are good aren't selling their advice to the public.

There's a lot to discuss about the vagaries of the stock market, but if we're going to continue on this journey of waking up, before we even discuss individual stocks, stock sectors, and stock indexes, we have some more deprogramming to do. I've already mentioned the need to turn off the television and close the magazines, but we need to look a little bit more at that. Then we're going to talk about what to do with your emotions and how you can best understand them so they play a key—but not overwhelming—role in your decision-making processes. First, let's look back at some of the worst prognostications of the last several decades, the ones that formed the basis of thought for many magazine subscribers in the last decade.

Boiling It Down

- Don't go down the rabbit hole of constantly buying individual stocks or day-trading. You probably don't have the time or the expertise. Stick with index funds and ETFs.

- If you must buy stocks, don't buy stocks and never sell them. If a stock is a long-term dog, sell it. The same goes for ETFs or other assets.

- You can't just forget about your stocks or any of your investments for months on end.

- Keep your costs low. Stay away from high-priced funds and watch out for big fees on investments.

- Simply investing 60 percent of your money in stocks and 40 percent in bonds is not enough diversification.

- Rebalancing your assets on a regular basis, holding bonds, and understanding your emotions will make you a better investor.

- Understand how much money you will need to retire.

Endnotes

[1] Federal Reserve Board, Survey of Consumer Finances, http://www.federalreserve.gov/pubs/oss/oss2/scfindex.html.

[2] Author interview.

[3] Mizuho Securities report.

[4] Spectrum Group, Mass Affluent Report 2009, www.spectrum.com.

[5] Jason Zweig, "Does Stock Market Data Really Go Back 200 Years?," *Wall Street Journal*, July 11, 2009.

[6] Author interview, 1999.

[7] Roger Ibbotson and Peng Chen, "Are Bonds Going to Outperform Stocks in the Long Run? Not Likely." Ibbotson Assoc., a Morningstar company, July 2009.

2

Advice to Ignore

"For better or for worse, the U.S. economy probably has to regard the death of equities as a near-permanent condition— reversible some day, but not soon."
Business Week's Aug. 13, 1979, "The Death of Equities" cover story

The most derided magazine cover of the last three decades, the one held up for the most ridicule (other than perhaps *Time* magazine's famous alteration of O. J. Simpson's mug shot), was *Business Week's* mid-1979 cover story, "The Death of Equities." It's been an article of faith that the story is Exhibit A in the long history of evidence for investors to consider media a contrarian indicator for market trends: If a leading publication says the rally is over, it's time to start buying. If stocks look cheap, according to *Smart Money* or *Kiplinger's* or worse yet, *Newsweek* or another general-interest publication, they're obviously expensive. (This goes triple if the stock market somehow lands on the cover of *Playboy* or *Golf Digest*.)

But the derision aimed at *Business Week's* famous cover story is somewhat misplaced. The article ran in 1979, and stocks didn't start to recover until 1982, after which they began a historic bull run that lasted 18 years. For three years, this article appeared astute and prescient. Considering current investing habits, where investors turn over their portfolio in a matter of weeks, three years might as well be a lifetime.

That's not to say the story got it right: It features its share of myopic pronouncements, particularly about the outlook for stocks (the article suggests Wall Street was unlikely to try to revive interest in equities through a promotional campaign because of the other investment possibilities that existed at that time).

The tone of the article suggested that a revival of equity interest was not likely, but the conditions *BW* said were necessary for a rebound came to pass. In the piece, the authors wrote that "to bring equities back to life now, secular inflation would have to be wrung out of the economy, and then accounting policies would have to be made more realistic and tax laws rewritten."[1]

Basically, that's what ended up happening. On some level, though, it's hard to blame the writers. Inflation was rampant in the late 1970s, and the political will to confront that had been missing at the Federal Reserve, the central banking authority in the U.S., for years. Notably, the article was published August 13, 1979—one week after the appointment of Paul Volcker to head the Federal Reserve. The previous chairman, G. William Miller, lasted just 17 months on the job and was deemed "the most partisan and least respected chairman in the Fed's history," according to veteran Federal Reserve watcher Steven Beckner, in his book *Back from the Brink: The Greenspan Years*. Miller and his predecessor, Arthur Burns, pursued policies that allowed inflation to rise, rather than reining it in. Volcker's efforts—raising rates into double-digit territory—finally broke the back of inflation. While the subsequent tenures of Alan Greenspan and Ben Bernanke garner mixed reviews, Volcker's reputation as a central banker is impeccable.

The *Business Week* article was wrong in many ways, but the popular view that its cover story could be heralded as a turning point in stocks is off the mark, too. At the very least, the *Business Week* article was attempting to dissect how inflation was ruining stock returns (it was) and how current fiscal and monetary policies were constraining capital investment (they were). They did at least point out that certain changes would have to come to pass for stocks to regain their mojo, and those changes did come to pass. Similarly, in 2010, for the stock market to put together a sustained advance based on something other than borrowed money, worrisome issues of inflation, debt burdens, and economic malaise will have to be combated.

Besides, if people want to point fingers at the media for poor predictions, there are much better, more recent examples! For one thing, at least *Business Week* did not advise investors on what stocks they should pick. Those that have done this in recent years, well, one would have made a fortune shorting against just about all of the names that came up. The best of these would be any major magazine that made a habit out of picking individual stocks over the last couple of decades, and in particular a pair of comically terrible predictions made by *Fortune* magazine and *Smart Money* magazine at the end of the century. The two magazines drew up lists of stocks to buy for the coming decade, and it's hard to imagine they could have made worse selections if they'd allowed chimpanzees to do the work for them.

The worst part about all of it is that these picks, on some level, have sensible, rational arguments behind them, and you'll find that in the stock market, the investments that frequently doom the most people are the ones that seem all the more plausible because of a company's unique position in a market, or because a certain sector of the economy appears poised to grow at a tremendous rate as the public warms to a new technology. Fad investments make suckers out of people, but not as many as those ideas that prove disastrous just because they seem so plausible.

Let's start with *Fortune* magazine, which in August 2000 put together a list of ten stocks to buy for the coming decade, with this whopper of a headline: "A few major trends will likely shape the next ten years. Here's a buy-and-forget portfolio to capitalize on them."[2] Buy and *forget*, they suggested. Not only were they so confident that these were the best picks out there, you could afford to *not even pay attention*. And you might ask, who would listen to such a thing? Well, plenty of people did, and plenty of people will again in the invariable next bull market, when such articles need to be ignored. But I digress—if you followed this advice, the only thing to forget about was *your money*. Table 2.1 shows *Fortune's* list, notable mostly for how horrid the picks turned out.

TABLE 2.1 *Fortune* **Magazine's List of "Ten Stocks to Last the Decade" in 2000**

Stock	Returns 7/19/00-12/31/09
Genentech	+153.04%
Oracle	-33.48%
UVN	-36.48%
Schwab	-45.73%
Viacom	-52.50%
Morgan Stanley Dean Witter	-59.59%
Nokia	-75.81%
Broadcom	-80.12%
Nortel Networks	-100%*
Enron	-100%**

Source for returns: Birinyi Associates Inc.
*Nortel entered bankruptcy protection in January 2009.
**Yes, *Fortune* really picked Enron.

There you have it. There's one winner in this group—Genentech, which did well due to breakthroughs in biotechnology. The list includes Morgan Stanley Dean Witter (ugh) and even worse, Enron, the energy company that turned out to be, more or less, a rigged trading operation. Overall, the portfolio dropped by 43 percent for the decade (if the stocks are equal-weighted), compared with the 24 percent drop in the S&P 500 index in this period of time.

Yet, *Fortune* magazine continues to publish picks of stocks every year, throwing out their best investment ideas without a real road map of how much to buy of each one, whether to divide one's portfolio up evenly, or when to take profits or sell outright (the magazine does a midyear update on the stocks, but that's it). The magazine, like other publications, has restrictions as it is not a registered investment advisory, so it can't constantly update its list or write recommendations each time something changes. Their track record invariably contains a number of years where the stocks they picked outpace the market, and then in other years, trail the broad averages, but there's no blueprint, no allocation to follow, and no accountability other than a year-end reckoning on how the picks did. (Is one expected to sell all of the positions at the end of the year and then buy the new ones? How does this work, exactly?) And for as much credibility as the magazine has as an investigative enterprise, there's no reason to expect it will have any ability to outdo the market in a long period of time. So why bother? They'd probably argue that there's an element of sport in all of it, but this is your money, and shouldn't be given over to the whims of a magazine editor.

They're not alone; other major investing publications have similar lists. And if it can be proven that supposed experts in the field—fund managers, institutional investors, and financial advisors—are lousy at picking individual stocks, well, the same can be said for journalists. Professional money managers are thought of as having high qualifications, but as we shall see, their returns tend to fail to match the long-term averages. But their track record is stellar when compared with those who are a few notches down on the totem pole in terms of qualifications—financial advisors, newsletter writers, and finally, journalists. This is not to deride the media, of which I am a proud member, but individual members of the Fourth Estate are notoriously poor at picking stocks, and their value is better put to use with investigative work of companies (think Bethany McLean, also of *Fortune*, paramount in exposing the accounting fiction that was Enron, which the editors believed was one of the best picks for the decade a couple of years earlier).

Smart Money's list published in late 1999[3] is likewise an amazing document to behold. It contains exactly two stocks that actually did well, like Monsanto, and then a handful of absolute portfolio killers: Citigroup, which was riding high in 1999 but imploded late in the decade; America Online, the product of one of corporate America's worst mergers, the marriage of AOL and Time Warner, which the latter is still trying to live down after years of wealth-destroying performance of its shares; and MCI WorldCom, the other accounting fiction of the decade that blew up a few years later, and somehow didn't make it into *Fortune*'s 2000 list of recommended stocks. Overall, a simple average of the portfolio—the surviving stocks, anyway—gives you an average return of minus 42 percent, just as bad as the *Fortune* list.

What's interesting as well is that the list published includes a column, next to the stock prices, of each issue's price-to-earnings ratio at the time. For the uninitiated, the price-to-earnings ratio measures a company's yearly earnings (let's call it $1 per share) and divides that into the share price (say, $20). It is one of the most commonly used ways to value stocks. Companies with higher growth expectations can command higher price-to-earnings ratios because investors can be reasonably assumed to pay more for stronger growth; those with lower expectations have lower ratios. On average, the S&P 500 has been around 16 for its lifespan. In the simplest explanation, a price-to-earnings ratio of a company that falls below its long-term average likely means the stock is undervalued. A P/E ratio that's above that potentially means the stock is overvalued.

That makes the P/E ratios of these selections even more ridiculous. The lowest? Citigroup, at 15.5 times earnings, which can be considered a reasonable valuation. Half of the ten stocks listed have P/E ratios above 40. That's far too high to be considered a potential growth candidate. The top P/E of 297.3 was Inktomi, a company that provided software for Internet service providers. On October 22, 1999, the stock closed at $103.06 a share—less than half its peak, which came later, at $241 a share in March 2000. In 2002, the company was acquired by Yahoo for a paltry $235 million, or $1.63 a share.

The list is shown in Table 2.2.

TABLE 2.2 *Smart Money's* "Ten Stocks for the Next Decade" in 2000

Stock	Ten-Year Return
Scientific-Atlanta	+56.47%
Monsanto	+21.37%*
Broadcom	-16.65%
Red Hat	-17.81%
America Online	-22.79%
Nokia	-51.11%
Citigroup	-90.15%
Inktomi	-96.8%
Nortel Networks	-100%
MCI WorldCom	-100%**

Data on Returns: Birinyi Associates Inc.

*Monsanto merged with Pharmacia & Upjohn in April 2000; the IPO off the remaining company was bought by Pfizer in April 2003.

**Yes, *Smart Money really* did pick MCI WorldCom.

So that's two winners, three stocks that did poorly but still stayed ahead of the S&P 500's dismal returns for that period, and five unmitigated disasters. It's further interesting that the two stocks that somehow made it into both lists published by *Fortune* and *Smart Money* are two of the worst investments: Nortel Networks and Broadcom.

The Nortel Flameout

Nortel stands as one of the great stock-market blowups of the last couple of decades. *Fortune* magazine, in its 2000 article touting Nortel as one of the stocks for the decade, quoted Steve Harmon, a "tech guru" who founded Zero Gravity Internet Group, saying that Nortel, based on its market share of optical networking systems, could "become the GE of technology the way they are operating." Of course, this was a decidedly 1990s view (magazines have since stopped quoting "tech gurus," for one).

The company, based in Toronto, was a spin-off of Bell Telephone Company of Canada, separating from its parent in 1895 because it wanted to build products other than telephones. It continued this way for decades, eventually producing telegraphic switchboards for military operations, and later pioneering a digital central office switch produced in the mid-1970s that served more than 100,000 office lines at once. And it became a huge player in the global fiber optic networking space in the mid-1990s.

But the stock price was clearly just not sustainable, something the editors of *Fortune* should have realized when this sentence was approved for publishing: "Like a lot of stocks in this sector, Nortel's isn't cheap. It trades at a P/E of around 114, bolstered by a 52-week gain of 250." The alarm bells should go off all over the place when reading that line. At the beginning of it, the author is rationalizing, saying its expensive profile is "like a lot of stocks" in the sector, which must somehow make it tolerable. Then he tells you the facts—a price-to-earnings ratio of 114, a mind-blowing number, as it had gained 250 percent in the last year. With the exception of stocks that are trading at 50 cents each, you just don't gain 250 percent in a year without consequences. In September 2000, Nortel had a market capitalization of $398 billion in Canadian dollars, or about $254 billion U.S., which accounted for one-third of the market cap of the entire Toronto Stock Exchange (when one company is the bulk of any market, it's a bad sign). By August 2002, the market cap had dropped to about $3.2 billion, and it continued to cascade from there, but not before CEO John Roth had sold his own stock options to net himself a profit of $86 million in 2000.

Broadcom's story is a bit less harrowing. For one thing, the company is still in existence, which gives it a leg up on Nortel, Enron, and WorldCom. So it's got that going for it. If you bought the stock when *Smart Money* recommended it, at $37.75 a share, you'd have lost money, but not your shirt. When *Fortune* recommended it, in August 2000, it was just about at its peak of $182 a share. The stock soldiers on, and is, like other big-cap technology stocks that dominated the market in the late 1990s, "dead money" for anyone stubborn enough to think they're going to be made whole after all these years, though most of those investors are long gone.

Momentum Investing and Popular Media

The *Smart Money* and *Fortune* covers tap into the fascination that exists with stock picking that isn't going to go away, no matter how bad a bear market comes to hammer the financially uneducated. Picking names out of a hat (which the *Wall Street Journal* famously did for years, looking at how a dartboard portfolio did against actual money managers) is interesting; it drives sales of magazines, and it provides investors with some kind of hope that they can accomplish the elusive goal that we fail at—to defeat the market's average, to come out in front, by getting a few investments right. When you think about it, trying to come up with a bunch of stocks that will outperform isn't much different than putting together your list of favorite sleepers in fantasy baseball or betting on which movie will make the most money in the summer movie season. But those bets don't form the basis of your retirement account, and random picking of stocks can, and that's a big mistake.

It gets truly dangerous when a particular stock or sector or market attracts the fascination of the popular media, which does tend to arrive at a story far after smart investors have already made a lot of money. Momentum drives this: Stocks that have been doing well for a period of months tend to continue to do well, and high-flying short-term gainers attract interest from less-informed investors in the marketplace, which helps stocks maintain an upward trend. An entire investing strategy, known as momentum investing, has flourished out of these tendencies; investors will follow stocks that show strong

upward trends and jump on the bandwagon, hoping to get off before
the stock inevitably falls. Eventually, such trends tend to stop, and
more seasoned investors abandon a stock as it becomes overvalued.
Without ready buyers to support a stock price, those who got in last
are the ones who get burned, and more often than not those are individual investors who have invariably read an article on a fascinating
new sector of the market that's going to be bigger than anyone can
imagine. The tendency for investors to follow the crowd was docu-
mented by three professors in the *Financial Services Review* in 2006.
They wrote that "professional analysts are successful with the
momentum strategy but the individual investors are not... momentum investing is not a viable strategy for individual investors."[4] The
professors looked at individuals and professionals who participated in
the WSJ Dartboard feature between 1999 and 2002, checking out
how they did with individual purchases.

They found that both groups—individuals and professionals—
focus on momentum stocks, those that are riding winning streaks, and
many pick stocks that had already doubled in the last six months. The
problem is that we are slower to catch on to such trends, and don't end
up grabbing those stocks until the upward trend is petering out. Is it so
far-fetched to think that leading investment magazines don't factor in
momentum when coming up with stocks to buy and "forget about" for
a decade? Looking back at the *Smart Money* list, Nortel had gained
250 percent in the last year as the authors had already noted. Broadcom's returns were strong when *Smart Money* recommended it, and it
was near a peak when *Fortune* suggested investors buy it. America
Online and Citigroup were giant conglomerates that had been through
substantial merger activity and were in the news on a daily basis.

There's not one stock in these two groups that anyone could
regard as an obscurity, which shows the power of momentum—
investor interest begets interest begets interest. You can't tell any
rational person that recommending high-flying stocks like World-
Com, Enron, Lucent, or Inktomi represents the carefully considered

advice of someone who spent days agonizing over such picks; more likely it was an attempt to latch onto something with momentum and pick out the names that seemed like they had the best chance of surviving another decade. And so for every instance in which you're considering a purchase of a sector (since we're not doing individual names here), an exchange-traded fund, or an investment in a particular country, you have to stop and think: Why am I buying this now? Am I getting in at a time before everyone else is? Or is it because I've just gotten this idea from a friend or a magazine noting great expectations? Have I done any research on this at all? Do I know anything about this industry?

The latter question—whether you know anything about the investment in question—is one that many people forgot during the tech bubble, and seemingly ignored during the financial bubble of the late 2000s as well. During this time, a frequent refrain from those who elected to largely stay away from the myriad tech companies springing up was this: "I don't understand what they do." That's an understandable rule; it's unwise to invest in businesses that one has a fundamental difficulty wrapping one's arms around.

But this term did not just refer to the stated aims of these companies—providing "solutions" for complex problems that a veteran investor did not know existed—but the money-making prospects of those companies. The Internet space exploded in those years, and hundreds of companies issued public offerings of stock before having established a clear path to profitability. From there came the rationalizations. Since these companies didn't make money, traditional ways of valuing them (by looking at their price and comparing it to expected earnings) were altered. Now it was acceptable to compare price to expected sales, even if profits weren't part of the picture, or to compare to "eyeballs"—the number of people expected to view a particular application. And so the phrase, "I don't understand what they do," became shorthand for those people who saw these investments and didn't see how, in any way, they could make money. The same started to be said of the banking stocks in the last part of the last decade, when the amount of leverage they had (that is, how much they had borrowed to make the money they were making) exceeded all reasonable boundaries and most of the unreasonable ones, too.

And yet it's a truism that stocks, in environments such as this, can kick the butts of all comers for a short period of time. They tend to become losers and revert to the market over a three- and five-year period, but for a year or so, irrational bets can run higher and higher. Professionals tend to be the ones who garner more of an advantage from big bets like this. How did they do? Pros in the 2006 Financial Services Review study ended up with a market-adjusted return of 8.28 percent, while readers lost 3.78 percent. The difference seems to stem partially from professionals' ability to herd in and out of stocks with positive and fading price momentum, something readers may be slower to get. They also may not be taking account of the same factors that professionals are, instead using strategies that rely "more exclusively on observed price increases. Such behavior may result in security selections that have experienced longer-term positive momentum and thus are closer to a reversal," they write. Basically, regular investors are seeing prices go up, and want to get in on that, period, and don't consider it beyond that.

Why do so many want to keep doing this? They want to get rich, quickly. That's why they continue to want to search for what one-time Fidelity fund manager Peter Lynch coined "10-baggers," stocks that absolutely explode, and can make an investor rich in a hurry (an early investor in Google, for instance). The Internet's reach and the deals offered by discount brokerages (150 free trades now!) engender this kind of approach among people, to glom onto a fad and try to ride it higher. But bad investments can destroy a portfolio, and if individuals are looking for a quick answer, this is a terrible way to go, particularly because of the lack of accountability inherent when magazines publish such lists. (If you bought those stocks as recommended by *Smart Money*, did you sell them all at the right time, if possible? Probably not.)

That's why those magazines have to be considered to be not much different than putting together lists of the best movies of the year, best books, top sporting events, or making prognostications about which football team will win the Super Bowl. It's just that those lists are meant mostly as fodder for conversation. A big magazine cover that splashes "Our Oscar Picks!" is geared to pique interest on the part of people who love lists and have an interest in movies—which is a ton of people—but it cannot be confused with actionable intelligence, as it really only translates into a guideline for $20 bets in the company Academy Awards pool. Such a blasé interpretation of a magazine's stock picks does not pass muster, not when people are constantly looking for an edge in the market, for that one idea that will push them out in front of everyone else.

And yet it continues. MoneySense, a Canadian personal finance Web site, in June 2009[5] decided to try its hand at ten stocks to pick for the coming decade, even acknowledging the dreadful record *Fortune* compiled by trying to put together a similar list. The MoneySense editors think they can succeed where *Fortune* failed; author Barbara Hawkins wonders what the *Fortune* editors "were smoking," pointing out that *Fortune* picked a handful of very expensive stocks, did not diversify widely, and bet on industries that were currently dominating the market. This is all true. MoneySense's own list intentionally looks for cheap companies, and so it found among them plane manufacturer Boeing and several other Dow industrials components—Microsoft, Johnson & Johnson, and Wal-Mart. This is admittedly a better approach, but only time will tell whether these names, seemingly sound ideas in a world obsessed with safety in 2009-2010, will turn out prescient in a decade. But the record is not good, even if the magazine wants to have it both ways with a self-aware acknowledgement that "this is a dangerous exercise" by pointing out the unreliability of such predictions, and then making the predictions anyway. What will Hawkins say in ten years if it turns out badly? Slough it off as an exercise in futility that was already destined to flounder?

Buy GM, But Don't Quote Us on That

The penchant for major investing publications to choose picks at the beginning of each year speaks, again, to the egalitarian nature of investing—that this is something everyone can practice, similar to journalism or home improvement, even if there are professionals who can do the job more effectively. It's possible that the gamelike nature of these picks could be considered harmless if they weren't followed, but they are weighed by investors making decisions about their money. What's more problematic is when publications write articles on end about how prevailing trends in the market are soon to come to a close (particularly bullish trends). This is part of the more contrarian nature of journalism, although of course such articles come as a result of research, which involves talking to market strategists, none of whom has a better idea than any other whether the market is going to rise or fall in coming months, because it is impossible to determine on most levels. But the stock in trade among members of the financial media is a need to be skeptical of prevailing trends—countless stories have been written casting doubt on the strength of the market's rally, or of its relative weakness. But the advice can be even more disastrous than a quixotic attempt to pick stocks for the next decade.

Case in point: *Barron's*, the weekly investing magazine, put together a June 2, 2008, cover story titled "Buy GM," referring to the beleaguered automotive company that was struggling to stay afloat.[6] In the piece, the author said the stock seemed suited mostly for investors with an appetite for risk and a strong stomach. "Despite the misery that the car maker is experiencing and might endure for another 12 to 18 months, such a wager ultimately should pay off," he wrote. The company was forced into bankruptcy early in 2009, and shareholders were wiped out.

Barron's had a similar clunker of a recommendation less than two months later. On July 21, they quoted Mark Boyar of Boyar Investments saying financial stocks were a "once in a generation" opportunity.[7] The article said "the brutal selloff in financial stocks— the worst for any major industry group since the technology bubble burst in 2000—could be over." But the financial stocks continued to crater, with many imploding in September 2008. Those that disappeared after this article appeared included Washington Mutual, Merrill Lynch, and Lehman Brothers, which *Barron's* noted was one of Boyar's favorites. But *Barron's* was confident in its prognosis, particularly with its assessment of regional banking institutions:

> "Regional banks, which had been pummeled until a sharp rebound that started Wednesday, have deposit bases that are so valuable that buyers of banks historically have paid sizable premiums to get them. Deposits now are being accorded little or no value throughout the banking industry as many institutions, including SunTrust Banks (STI), Marshall & Ilsley (MI), Comerica (CMA), Wachovia (WB) and Zions Bancorporation (ZION) trade around their tangible book values—a conservative measure that excludes goodwill and other intangible assets."

This conservative measure was so compelling that regional banks were mashed through the rest of 2008—the Keefe, Bruyette & Woods Regional Banking Index lost 22 percent that year, and when the lion's share of the stock market posted a big turnaround in 2009, regional banks remained the worst performers as lending outside major institutions continued to stall, despite rock-bottom interest rates. That index dropped an additional 24 percent in 2009. Rising provisions to cover bad loans and expected deterioration in commercial real estate socked the regional commercial banks, and Marshall & Ilsley was the S&P's worst performer for the year.

"How much did *Barron's* cost you? $5? That's probably about how much that advice is worth," said Jeff Rubin of Birinyi Associates. "If something changes four or five months out there's no guarantee you'll have an update. They can't go back and say, 'sell this stock.' That's not what they do—their job is to sell advertising."[8]

Barron's endeavors to maintain a track record of how it is doing, listing all of the stocks they talked about positively or negatively in a particular year, and then averaging their performance against their varying benchmarks. For some reason, disaster picks like the June 2008 recommendation of General Motors are not included (this makes very little sense—the company's cover story was titled "Buy GM"). The banks are also not included in the 2008 tally. Even so, the magazine's track record is about as spotty as any other magazine. Its bullish picks in 2007 on average were down 23 percent through April 28, 2010, compared with a 15.8 percent loss for the average benchmark, according to *Barron's*. They're faring a bit better with 2008 picks, up 6 percent compared with a 0.02 percent loss for the benchmark, and the 2009 picks are up a handsome 41.9 percent, while the benchmarked average index is up just 30.7 percent. But, really, big deal—it's not been anywhere close to long enough to really determine whether these picks worked.[9]

Barron's also has a track record of its bearish picks, which an investor is presumably supposed to use to build short positions, but those picks also have a mixed record. Its 2009 bearish picks are up, on average, 17.8 percent, trailing the index average of 33.4 percent by a long shot; the bearish 2008 picks are up 7.2 percent, better than the 1 percent gain in the average index. The 2007 bearish picks have done terribly, falling 28.4 percent compared with a 13.4 percent drop in the index average, according to *Barron's* data.

A long-standing feature in *Barron's* was the roundtable, a year-end gathering of various investment managers to discuss picks for the coming year, and naturally, these ideas and predictions had a few gems hidden in them, but on the whole were rather suspect. Most of those who were summoned to participate in this roundtable, such as Ellen Harris or Joe Neff, appeared year after year. The roundtable continues to this day, with noted strategists Mario Gabelli, Bill Gross, and Abby Joseph Cohen of Goldman Sachs appearing in the vaunted articles. And this isn't to say these strategists, taken together, do not have some good ideas, but in general, so many are so far from being on the market that it becomes pointless to continue to follow one personality.

The individual desire to break out of the pack has supported another class of those proffering investment advice that rank, in terms of cost, somewhere below hedge funds and brokerage research and above free online advice and magazines, and that's the newsletter business. Mark Hulbert, editor of the *Hulbert Financial Digest* and a writer for MarketWatch.com and the *New York Times*, tracks the industry closely, and says he has a similar conclusion as many others—that most cannot beat the market, saying that it's "a dismal industry, and there's no evidence people are getting any better at it."[10] He estimates that there are anywhere from one to two million subscribers to newsletters, which would make the industry a $100 million to $200 million business, a lucrative one for those who attract a lot of subscribers as a result of their picks.

"Some have beaten the market over time, but the issue is not that: We know from the odds, one of five will beat the market over a period, but will the one of five in one period be the same that beat it in the previous period?" he asks. Hulbert looked at 200 different model portfolios covering the 2007-2009 bear market and found that while there were some that completely obliterated a passive index fund during the bear market (as the S&P 500 fell 50 percent), looking at the five-year period turned those results around. Just 11 of these model portfolios set up by newsletter writers made money during the bear market, which is great, but those same writers tended to lose money during the raging bull market that preceded the downturn. As a result, they averaged a gain of 1 percent annualized in the five-year period that ended when the bear ended, which isn't so hot, especially as the index fund managed a 0.9 percent annualized gain.

Some news magazines, in addition to recommending stocks, try their hand at mutual fund ideas too—the shelves of newsstands are littered with monthly issues suggesting the "best funds to buy" at any given moment. Motley Fool, a popular Web site devoted to puncturing investment myths, put it best in 2000, saying cheekily that "scientific marketing surveys and focus group testing have determined that magazines with covers that read 'Index Funds: Still The Best Choice!!!' every single month really wouldn't sell as well as magazines that promise 'Our BRAND NEW 10 Best Mutual Funds To Buy RIGHT NOW!' Sad, but true."[11]

What's worrisome—and true-blue journalists would deny this influence—is that many major publications write articles that mention funds that also happen to be heavy advertisers in those monthly and weekly tomes.

In a 2005 article, professors Jonathan Reuter and Eric Zitzewitz found a significant relationship between a fund company's advertising expenditures and the chances that its funds will be recommended in leading personal finance magazines. "The robustness of the correlation leads us to conclude that the most plausible explanation is the causal one, namely, that personal finance publications bias their recommendations—either consciously or subconsciously—to favor advertisers," they wrote.[12]

This allegation would not sit well with the editors of the major publications in question—*Money* magazine, *Smart Money*, and *Kiplinger's Personal Finance*—but these magazines depend on advertising revenue from the mutual fund industry, which accounts for anywhere from 15 percent to nearly 30 percent of their advertising sales. (By contrast, Reuter and Zitzewitz found that the *Wall Street Journal* and *New York Times* derived about 4 percent and 1 percent, respectively, of their revenue from mutual fund industry ads.)

And the funds mentioned are benefiting as well. They found that positive articles in personal finance magazines and *Consumer Reports* are "associated with an economically significant seven to eight percent increase in fund size over the next 12 months, while a positive mention in the *New York Times* is associated with a 15 percent increase," they wrote.

But as we see later, mutual fund investors fall far short of the returns advertised by the funds themselves, because we are buying those funds at exactly the wrong times—and we're doing so because of mentions in the media, Morningstar's vaunted star ratings system, and advertisements. And it's not as if journalists follow these recommendations. *Fortune* itself admitted this with an article in 1999 entitled "Confessions of a Former Mutual Funds Reporter." In this, the anonymous author says that reporters "seem delighted in dangerous sectors like technology," but "by night, we invest in sensible index funds." In sum, the reporter writes, "we were preaching buy-and-hold marriage while implicitly endorsing hot-fund promiscuity. The better we understood the industry, the sillier our stories seemed."[13]

There's a reason for this. Publications need a story angle to make a story worthwhile; the media is supposed to inform and illuminate as well as broaden one's knowledge. Writing about a topic or fund nobody knows about meets those criteria without a doubt—too bad it's an awful method for stock picking.

This isn't done out of a desire to curry favor with advertisers—most publications worth their salt head off their advertisers' entreaties when it comes to coverage—but it does suggest that magazines aren't looking much further than their own pages for ideas. As a result, it suggests, worryingly, that publications could be gearing their coverage around what will sell ads, or even worse, favorable coverage of mutual funds and investment advisories crops up as a result of heavy ad dollars. And the lack of knowledge that journalists have—the "Confessions" article says reporters were instructed to look to recent returns and hot sectors—makes advice that can be considered suspect at best even more conflicted, and therefore basically useless.

Ultimately, the better one understands this industry, the sillier *all* of the arguments for a particular purchase—be it a stock, commodity, ETF, or fund—seem, unless one is arguing in favor of the lowest-cost view. Americans in general tend to be slaves to bargains when it comes to electronics, apparel, home furnishings, automobiles, and even household goods. We buy massive jars of mayonnaise because it costs less per pound than the smaller, more sensibly sized jar. (Okay, that's perhaps not the strongest example.) But when it comes to investments, there's still a belief among many that the edge can only be found through additional expenditures—how else would the hedge fund industry, which charges a 2 percent management fee and 20 percent of the profits, manage to thrive as it has?

In retrospect, *Business Week* may have deserved more pillorying for the cover story it published in mid-1997. You'd think, 15 years after having been proved terribly wrong with an article about the death of the stock market, *BW*'s editors would have steered clear of another grand pronouncement. And yet on June 15, 1997, the magazine produced a piece called "How Long Can This Last?" which led off by asking, "could it get any better than this?" The magazine leaned on the then-popular "productivity miracle" argument, one that suggested further automation was making workers more productive, and therefore large companies more viable. This, would, in turn, lead to enhanced returns for years to come.[14]

Once again, *Business Week* had it largely incorrect, as the productivity thesis was largely disproved some years down the road, but this article is less egregious in that it does not attempt to convince readers of the inherent inferiority of equities (or their superiority, as it was in the late 1990s). It's more a dissertation on the economic environment, not the market, so it's less of a ringing endorsement of the folly of buying stocks based on magazine covers.

Talking Dartboards

If the stock market has been turned into a spectator sport as much as any other game—be it poker, baseball, or horse racing—then James Cramer, the former hedge fund manager who hosts a wildly successful program on CNBC, is sort of the Ryan Seacrest of the business media community, less good-looking, but nowhere near as bland. His appeal has a few aspects. For one, he's exceedingly smart, and it's hard not to see that. Second, his enthusiasm is unbridled, and investors pick up on that and convince themselves that they can make the kind of money that he made in the investing world for a number of years. Third, his approach is simple—the world is your oyster, buy whatever stocks you see fit (provided you do research, which he talks about in his book). Who wouldn't find a "lightning round," where Cramer opines on a handful of stocks in a few seconds that are thrown at him by readers, appealing? He spouts so much information in such a short period of time, it's no wonder he was once referred to by Jon Stewart as a "dartboard that talks." But there's only one of him. To some extent—if you read his writings—he knows this, but on his show he's doing his best to entertain. On some levels that's a cop-out as people pay attention to his advice, and the stocks he picks tend to exhibit the same kind of "momentum effect" that stocks recommended by magazines tend to show.

A Northeastern University study in 2006 found that his picks tend to underperform the market, though a later, updated version of this study in 2009 showed better results. His portfolio gained 31.75 percent compared with a gain of about 18 percent for the S&P 500 for the period from July 2005 to December 2007.[15]

Good stuff, right? Now, of course, the cost of trading has to be taken into account. Assuming a flat rate of $9.99 per trade, that drops the portfolio's performance to a gain of 22.42 percent, which is still ahead of the S&P's passive 18.72 percent, according to Northeastern's study. Now taxes have to be accounted for as well, and that would reduce the take further. Using certain other factors, such as investment risk, his portfolio fell short of the S&P 500 in 2006, but slightly outperformed in 2007. Furthermore, a two-year period is too small of a sample to really know whether a particular investor has real stock-picking skill. Cramer has said in the past—and in his book—that unless investors have the time to spend on researching stock positions, investing in this way is not a good idea. (There's no doubt it works for him—it's his lifeblood. But nobody else is Jim Cramer.)

Again, though, a similar conclusion can be reached when taking into account all of the factors involved in active trading and relying on the recommendations of others: That the returns advertised by Cramer, by mutual fund companies, or newsletters are not what they seem because the takeaway is that much less due to trading costs and taxes. Of course, that's not what's advertised, and media coverage of the Cramer study focused on the simple, easy to understand numbers that suggest he has some skill at picking stocks.

What's inarguable, and more dangerous, is the influence Cramer (and other prominent analysts) have on stocks in general. The Northeastern paper finds that stocks mentioned as a "buy" by Cramer tend to get a bump of about 2 percent on the next day of trading after his "Mad Money" show airs the previous evening. Over time, the influence of those recommendations wanes, but this "Cramer Effect" is something that conforms to what others have written about the impact of analyst recommendations on stocks. CNBC anchor Maria Bartiromo for years began the morning with a litany of updated recommendations from various prominent Wall Street analysts, but those recommendations were then "quickly reflected in stock prices through client actions, before the mass investing public comes to know about the opinions (second-hand information). Thus, from the perspective of the average investor, analyst opinions qualify as second-hand information," write the professors at Northeastern.

CNBC has become a bit smarter in recent years in the aftermath of the technology wreck. Investment gurus who appear on the show come armed with disclosures that appear onscreen, and they have to let viewers know whether they have long or short positions in the shares mentioned. But the focus is rarely on whether previous picks have worked out, and the horse-race nature of the coverage, namely, which stock is winning? Discussion of longer-term issues are reserved for the likes of Suze Orman, who, on a weekly basis, advises people to save their money and be smart, the kind of advice that doesn't bring in viewers during the week. Her show is on Saturdays. She is a best-selling author and has tons of followers, so the market for sound, boring advice isn't completely barren.

So turn off CNBC and try to stay focused on the long term. Rob Arnott, founder of Research Affiliates, which manages more than $50 billion in assets and is based in Newport Beach, California, tells a funny story about just what constitutes long term in the world of financial television. "I was being interviewed once on long-term forward looking returns, and was suggesting that [stocks] would be better than bonds, but not drastically, and the host said, 'But look, the market has risen 140 points in the time we've been talking,' and I had to resist bursting out laughing, because five minutes is not long term," says Arnott. "It was quite a visceral example of the short-termism when people think about investing. It is treated as a sporting event and as a game and it does have enormous impact on people's lives late in life."[16]

Boiling It Down

- Take the financial press with a big, big spoonful of skepticism. The media's track record is as bad as, or worse than, many professional investors.

- Don't get caught up in the excitement offered by Jim Cramer. If you're so determined to buy individual stocks, make sure you understand the perils—even the ones he points out—before proceeding.

- Before you make moves in your portfolio as a result of the excitement on television, make sure that what you're about to do meets your long-term goals. Are you considering changes just because the market has gotten a bit jumpy and the press even more so? Take a deep breath.

Endnotes

[1]"The Death of Equities: How Inflation Is Destroying the Stock Market," *Business Week*, August 13, 1979.

[2] David Rynecki, "10 Stocks to Last the Decade," *Fortune*, August 14, 2000.

[3]"10 Stocks for the Next Decade," *Smart Money*, October 1999.

[4]Glenn Pettengill, Susan Edwards, and Dennis Schmitt, "Is Momentum Investing a Viable Strategy for Individual Investors?" *Financial Services Review* 15 (2006), 181-197,

[5]"Ten Stocks for the Next Ten Years," MoneySense, http://www.moneysense.ca/2009/08/13/10-stocks-for-the-next-10-years/.

[6]Vito Racanelli, "Buy GM: General Motors' turnaround could accelerate in coming years, driving handsome gains for bold stockholders," *Barron's*, June 2, 2008.

[7] Andrew Bary, "What to Bank On," *Barron's*, July 21, 2008.

[8]Author interview.

[9]Barron's Online, http://online.barrons.com/stockpicks.

[10]Author interview.

[11]The Motley Fool, http://www.fool.com/mutualfunds/indexfunds/indexfunds01.htm.

[12]Jonathan Reuter and Eric Zitzewitz, "Do Ads Influence Editors? Advertising and Bias in the Financial Media," *Quarterly Journal of Economics*, August 2005.

[13]"Confessions of a Former Mutual Fund Reporter," *Fortune*, April 1999.

[14]Michael Mandel, Keith Naughton, Greg Burns, and Stephen Baker, "How Long Can This Last?," *Business Week*, June 15, 1997.

[15]Paul J. Bolster and Emery A. Trahan, "Investing in Mad Money: Price and Style effects," *Financial Services Review* 18 (2009), 69-86.

[16]Author interview.

3

Love Your Emotions, Don't Trade Them

"They used to say about the Bourbons that they forgot nothing and they learned nothing, and I'll say about the Wall Street people, typically, is that they learn nothing, and they forget everything."
Benjamin Graham, 1976, *Financial Analysts Journal*

About 30 years ago, a study was undertaken looking at the driving habits of people in Sweden and the United States, and participants were polled specifically on how well they thought of themselves as drivers. More than 80 percent of drivers in the U.S. considered themselves above average. A similar survey taken five years later found a similar conclusion, with four out of five believing their skills exceeded that of the average driver.

A similar dynamic exists in people's opinions of the U.S. Congress. For years, Congress as an institution has had abysmal ratings, ranging somewhere around a 20 percent approval rate. Yet when election season rolls around, most representatives are elected in a walk, with some facing little more than token opposition. Approval rates of 20 percent would suggest the opposite should occur, but people in general tend to remain more sympathetic to their own representative than the institution as a whole.

This kind of cognitive dissonance—identified as something called illusory superiority—can be viewed in the stock market as well, in the guise of investors who believe that they are superior traders than the average participant in markets. But it isn't possible for 85 percent of the investing public to be a better-than-average investor; the zero-sum-game nature of the market means that everyone who makes gains is being offset by someone who is losing money. We think we can outsmart the markets, but the ability to do so over an extended period of time is exceedingly rare. This belief drives plenty of decisions in the stock market, particularly in this era of active trading, when share turnover on the New York Stock Exchange surpasses 100 percent (that is, most fund managers don't hold any one stock for an entire year, turning over the entire portfolio within a 12-month period. And these are the managers supposedly trying to invest your money for the long term; so much for that.)

The generalized attitude we have—that we, somehow, will be able to avoid the pitfalls that so many other individuals fall into on a daily basis—is what helps produce volatility and allows savvier types to capitalize on the mistakes made by individuals, which are usually borne of emotion.

Most market professionals with only a modicum of understanding of behavioral science would tell you to "ignore your emotions." But only computers and robots can do that, and computers gave us Long-Term Capital Management and excessive algorithmic trading that helped merely bad days turn into cascading losses in the summer and fall of 2008. Program trading, particularly high-frequency traders, were what gave us the "flash crash" in May of 2010, when major stocks briefly were quoted at a penny a share and the market lost 9 percent of its value in a matter of minutes. Excessive reactions to emotions can be killers for individual investors, but a person cannot divorce himself from his emotions entirely—sometimes they are sending out strong signals that it is indeed time to change course.

"You're constantly sitting in front of a screen having [the market] declare whether you're smart or not," says Denise Shull, president of Trader Psyches, a consulting firm that helps investors understand their emotional reactions and how they can use them, rather than try to pretend they don't exist. "The market goes right to our core of feeling good about ourselves or about our futures rather than not feeling good about ourselves or the futures...it does this in a way that nobody else does."[1]

The emotional, or gut-level responses that we have to developing situations in the market manifest themselves in a few basic, repeated mistakes. Among them:

- People hold onto their losers and sell their winners, rather than doing the opposite, as they should.
- Investors buy into sectors that have been performing well for a long period of time and carry a certain cachet, rather than ignoring such overvalued investments.
- People ignore their first, and best, instincts when it comes to a failing investment, Shull says, and only react when the weight of doing nothing becomes so loathsome that it starts to make them feel sick.

Market Meltdowns and Mental Breakdowns

The good news is that most of these emotional responses to developments in the market can be fought through a disciplined approach to investing that allows for little deviation. This is why professionals refer to a "sell discipline," because it implies a regimented set of rules that cannot be ignored. Individuals often lack this, and so they go with mantras that have been absorbed that are not practiced, such as the much-discussed "buy for the long term" aphorism. Long-term investing is a fine approach, but only if an investor is willing to hold firm, rather than react to the short-term vagaries of what is happening in the equity market.

A number of people I spoke to in recent months talked of their experiences leading to the meltdown in the markets in late 2008. Some of them were smart enough to see problems developing earlier in the year, a few months after the market peaked in October 2007.

They thought about selling shares, but elected not to, and often their original instinct was countermanded with a phone call to a trusted advisor (a brokerage representative or independent advisor) who counseled against making such a move because markets "tend to always come back." While markets do, eventually, come back, it can help to avoid such bear markets if at all possible, even if one sets high bars to clear when deciding whether to sell or not: say, losses of 20 percent. Set a rule for yourself that when you are down 20 percent, you sell. Even that would have saved many an investor's hide in the nasty, protracted bear market of 2007-2008. If individuals had put such a rule in place, they would have cut their losses because they would have had to follow it. They didn't—so any explanation that seemed plausible (the subprime problems will be "contained," the banking system isn't going to melt down)—was enough to assuage many people, including those of you who wanted to believe things would be okay if you didn't do anything.

However, the primary word from investment advisors did not tend to suggest lightening up on holdings to reflect a client's concern. Instead, they were told, more or less, not to worry about it, because markets will rebound eventually. But of course you should worry about it! It's your money! Just as the advisor is worried about his well-being (which involves keeping as much of your assets as possible), so should you be worried about your position, too.

And here we come to another part of the deprogramming process: Understanding when to trust your own emotions, for one, and to reject investment advice that a broker's parrot could have memorized and repeated to you, ad nauseam. For many people, the very idea of losing money is anathema—so when you're confronted with the fact that your portfolio is staring you in the face, with 20 percent losses across the board, you want to believe that these losses aren't real. You tell yourself the losses didn't really happen because you didn't sell your stocks, and therefore they're just "paper" losses. (Do people feel this way about gains? Of course not. Gains are always tangible; losses don't count, sort of like how people rationalize going off their diets by saying the cookies they're eating don't count because they're not sitting down at a table to eat them, or some other silly notion.)

Invariably many of these investors ended up selling, getting out of their portfolio at the worst possible time—when their emotional state was most frayed, and when they had become completely divorced from the reality of the market. By this time, their response to the advisor is probably one of visceral hatred—and they're getting out of stocks to save their hide and stick it to the jerk who didn't have any real insight despite having an education in these matters. It's those times that professional money managers (good ones, anyway) scoop up what they regard as undervalued stock. And now, unlike before, when your losses were on paper, those 30 or 40 percent losses *are* real, and they could have been minimized.

Certain psychological responses to certain developments are understandable. People don't like to lose money, and they particularly don't like to lose money that they believed, based on a paper statement of stock holdings, was rightfully theirs, even though those profits were ephemeral. "When you have a paper profit but then you've lost that profit, that is a harder fear for people to handle than [simply] losing money," says Trader Psyches President Denise Shull. Essentially, investors are more willing to accept or rationalize an investing loss if it never made money—a stock purchased at $20 that then falls off to $5 before the investor sells it produces a less psychologically traumatic response than the stock that goes from $20 to $50 and then back to $5. That's because the latter scenario introduces regret, and Shull says the fear of regret is stronger than the fear of losing money.

The way such situations play out manifest themselves in the aftermath of bear markets, particularly bear markets in a particular sector that has been hit harder than the rest. The Nasdaq Stock Market rocketed to an all-time high in March 2000 before succumbing and losing more than 75 percent of its value, but in the period before the index finally hit bottom in 2003, there were a series of short rallies that boosted that index by 10 to 20 percent but were ultimately done in by further selling pressure. But some of the thinking behind the rallies following the great tech wreck came about as investors tried to rationalize earlier losses and convince themselves using a fallacy that a once-high stock price is a benchmark that can be referenced further down the road. (Often these rallies were built on the losses of others—a 2004 research report points out that investors tend to shy away from repurchasing stocks that they have lost money in. However, investors also tend to gravitate to "the subset of stocks that catch their attention,"[2] and that generally includes those stocks that are in the news.

As a result, people who have been involved heavily in buying and selling the technology sector might have continued to buy in that area, but instead of buying a money-losing JDS Uniphase they moved on to Juniper Networks or some other "related" stock because it was cheap. Once-strong stocks that collapsed bounced back for a time as investors decided to jump back in, but the gains didn't hold. That's the case for large-cap tech such as Microsoft, which is treading water years after hitting a peak, and smaller names like Broadcom or JDS Uniphase, which are still nowhere near their previously lofty heights.

"Getevenitis" Disease

There are a great many hackneyed clichés spoken in the market—within them, there are a few truths. One that many investors cling to, at least in their mind, is this: "Let your winners run, and sell your losers." It's a time-honored tool of portfolio management, but most investors screw this up, and end up doing the opposite—selling their winners and hanging onto the losers. "People treat losses differently than they treat gains," says hedge fund manager Eric Crittenden. "We're hard-wired to crave positive feedback, so we like to book gains. But we're willing to be optimistic when sitting on losses."[3] This, he says, comes as a result of investors' belief in their own judgment: If a company is a strong company, has good fundamentals and solid earnings, consistent, steady losses in the stock serve as a challenge to one's intellect. "When we get a gain, we're allowed to crow about its success and it is proof we were right," he says, but losses create an opposite effect. Since investors believe that they have not been proven correct or incorrect until the actual sale of shares is made (just as paper gains are just that, so are paper losses, as the rationalization goes), they can continue to believe their theories will come out ahead in the market. Barry Ritholtz, the author of *Bailout Nation* and chief investment officer at Fusion IQ, has the perfect rejoinder to this thinking: "Do you want to be right, or do you want to make money?"[4]

Unfortunately, investors are at times psychologically more inclined toward being right. Berkeley professor Terrence Odean found this to be the case more than ten years ago, finding that people tend to sell winners and buy stocks that have been performing less well. Instead of selling winners and pocketing the cash, they sell and buy...worse stocks! But those who held onto their winners instead of buying past losers exceeded the market average by 2.4 percentage points, and bested the losers by 3.4 percentage points. The motivations for doing so relate in part to an aversion to paying taxes by selling winners (gains not yet realized aren't taxed).[5]

Still, investors are predisposed to hold onto losers—what's called the disposition effect, which was coined in 1985 by Meir Statman and Hersh Shefrin when they began applying behavioral science to the stock market. They found that investors go through a series of mental calculations when it comes to buying and selling shares that leads them to make the wrong move—letting losers ride—instead of selling them when they should. Why would they do this? Because there's always the possibility that the stock rebounds, and if it does, an investor can "just break even," or perhaps recoup a bit of a purchase with a profit. However, there's also the chance that the stock can go lower, but in these cases, researchers have found that investors, when given the choice of letting it ride or accepting the smaller loss, tend to let it ride.

There's a term for this: "getevenitis disease," or get even-itis, coined by author and investment strategist LeRoy Gross, and he noted that this disease "has probably wrought more destruction on investment portfolios than anything else." While investors wait around for the stock in question to recover its original loss, the stock continues to drop—witness the slow destruction of investor capital in shares of General Motors, Citigroup, Nortel Networks, and scores of other companies that steadily deteriorated even though some held out hope that there would be a recovery.

Sometimes this aversion to loss—and the willingness to gamble further to avoid those losses—has devastating results, and not just for individual investing accounts. One of the most famous examples in recent years was in 1995, when derivatives trader Nick Leeson caused his employer, Barings Bank, to go bust as a result.

Leeson originally was profiting as a result of unauthorized trading in derivatives, but over time, he started losing money. He started to hide those trades, and instead of realizing those losses by selling—and admitting them to his employer—he made a series of even more complicated bets to try to recover his losses. Perhaps he was suffering from "getevenitis" himself. He eventually fled his home base of Singapore in February 1995, and Barings was declared insolvent a few days later. He was arrested a few weeks later, and his losses came to $1.4 billion. His comments, however, illustrate the disposition effect perfectly, as he said he "gambled on the stock market to reverse his mistakes and save the bank."

When it comes to actualizing losses, that is, selling shares at a loss, regret enters into the equation also: Just as a stock that's held in one's portfolio that carries a loss is not actualized until you go ahead and sell it, there's regret to making that decision—and not making an active choice to sell the stock at a gain or loss keeps people from feeling that regret. (When someone sells a stock at a loss they open themselves to the possibility of regret if the stock should rebound; when someone sells a stock for a gain, and then sees the stock go further, they are likely to repurchase it, in part because of regret of not having continued to hold the shares.) But here's the thing: Choosing not to decide still constitutes a choice, and if you think you can avoid regret by not actually making a sale, you'll feel differently if that asset you own falls by 30 percent out of nowhere.

By now you're probably admitting to having committed such an act at some point in the past: It's those moments when you say, "If only I hadn't sold that stock then," or "If only I'd bought the shares when I thought about it." I'm not trying to be a behavioral coach, but the process of investment is too complex and involves too many factors to allow regrets to dominate one's thinking. Instead, one needs to understand that such feelings are going to crop up in the course of buying certain funds or using a certain allocation strategy, and discipline can help reduce the risks of depending too much on emotion. But those emotions cannot be ignored: In fact, they are in some ways even more important to the decision of purchases, Shull argues. "Let's say you've invested in something that's gone up, and then it has pulled back," she says. "It could be that the fundamental situation has changed, and it could just be a good time to cut your losses. If people just were able to become aware of their feelings around that, it would save a lot of people a lot in their retirement accounts."

There are ways to get around this. Although this book does not advocate buying individual equities, it does advocate buying asset classes, funds, and possibly sectors. Those who seek to take a more active approach—that is, beyond just rebalancing yearly through an automatic selection (if your 401k plan has this)—should seek to step back and justify their purchases. If they're sticking to a disciplined asset allocation (60-40 or what-have-you), the discipline should be maintained instead of changing your guidelines to take advantage of a new opportunity.

Longtime Fidelity manager Peter Lynch advocated recording his thoughts on different companies, keeping notebooks that contained information on holdings. Hedge fund manager Julian Robertson reportedly quizzed associates in the hallways as to why they were buying a particular stock. Can your purchases be justified? If not, why not?

Fred Dickson, longtime market strategist at D. A. Davidson & Co., in Lake Oswego, Oregon, says individual investors often enter the markets with what seem like reasonable strategies, but are too quick to abandon them as things get difficult. "I think individual investors tend to come into the market intrigued by owning individual stocks and they have a basis of discipline for buying, and it'll work for a while," he says. "They lose the discipline along the way and when mistakes start happening, they abandon a sound strategy."[6] The inability to cope with making mistakes is compounded in a volatile market, especially after investors spent years living in a world where stocks didn't go down all that much, and the daily to-and-fro of stocks was easy to deal with. The last ten years have been very difficult for all of us, and giving yourself a few rules to work with will help you deal with those inevitable moments where you're frightened beyond belief.

Following the Herd

The herd mentality often spoken about in markets also revolves largely around regret or rather, the expectation of regret. Bubbles are borne out of this behavior. It's true that without a real investment behind it (okay, maybe not in the case of Pets.com), investors won't be expected to jump on board a speculative idea. But the idea that one has missed out on something is a powerful motivator for individuals, mutual fund companies, institutions, and large corporations as well: Many a mistake made during the massive financial crisis, the thing that doomed a particular institution, was a bet on a particular subset of the company's business that had previously only accounted for part of the business, but suddenly looked attractive, in part because other investors were making a mint in a particular area.

Washington Mutual became one of the biggest victims of the sub-prime mortgage lending crisis in part because the company decided to increase its exposure in 2007, when the tide was already turning for this troubled sector of the housing market.

The effects can often be more dangerous for the company that gets into an area with even less expertise (WaMu was already a large mortgage company in its own right). Merrill Lynch & Co., the gigantic retail brokerage, elected to get into the subprime industry in late 2006, buying the First Franklin mortgage origination business from National City Bank of Cleveland for $1.3 billion. First Franklin was founded in 1981 and in 1994, decided to start serving the "nonprime" market, that is, those buyers who had poorer credit ratings and therefore, a greater chance of defaulting on their mortgages. Eventually National City bought the company, and the purchase helped National City become the sixth-largest mortgage originator by 2003.

Merrill Lynch came into the picture in 2006. They bought the business for $1.3 billion even though, as an article on MarketWatch.com noted, subprime loans had "become riskier as the housing market has begun falling faster than expected and as defaults have started rising." They noted that David Daberko, National City's CEO, had warned at a conference a few weeks prior to the Merrill announcement in September that "he had seen a marked increase in first-payment defaults on loans." One year later, the purchase was in tatters, and the horrendous purchase was part of what crippled Merrill Lynch, which brokered a deal to be sold to Bank of America Inc. on the fateful weekend in mid-September 2008 when Lehman Brothers went bankrupt and American International Group became a ward of the state. Merrill made a number of stupid decisions during the financial crisis, but their ownership of terrible mortgages originated by First Franklin, and additionally, the ownership of loan obligations created from a pool of subprime loans, was a big part of what doomed the franchise.

So it's not just individuals that make bad decisions based on the madness of others in the crowd—big-time moneymakers do the same, which should call into question their ability to provide wise counsel to you in your financial decisions. Still, individuals remain among the worst offenders when it comes to latching onto a rally that has by then run its course. Data from the Investment Company Institute shows individuals continued to buy heavily into equity funds well into 2007, only beating a hasty retreat in late 2008 when the market melted down. (The two worst months for outflows were in September and October 2008, which of course turned out to be reasonably solid buying opportunities.) "People have a fear of missing out—that's really the fear of regret in the future, and that's really the fear behind bubbles," Shull says. Investors buy Google "because everyone else is buying Google, and that keeps working until the last person buys Google."

One of the more memorable examples of this mentality took place at the end of the previous decade. This was the time period when all investors wanted were technology and Internet-related stocks, and the mutual fund industry adeptly decided to capitalize on it. Investors flocked to the Munder NetNet Fund, a popular fund offering exposure to Internet stocks. This fund ballooned in size amid stellar performance thanks to the dot-com bubble. The fund posted returns of about 175 percent in 1999 and soon had more than $11 billion in assets by the spring of the next year—just as the market peaked. It then lost a ton in the next few years, losing 54 percent in 2000, 48 percent in 2001, and 45 percent in 2002. Since its inception in August 1996, the shares have returned an average 7.66 percent annualized, while the class C shares (which have a different expense ratio) have averaged just a 1.27 percent gain since inception in November 1998—even closer to the top of the bubble.

The fund underwent a pair of name changes, first to the Munder Internet Fund and then to the Munder Growth Opportunities Fund, no doubt trying to outrun its history. And even more recently fund executives talk of the misunderstanding that investors have when it comes to Munder, and how clients continued to complain about the fund as the management company tried to find more investors. But this goes back to investors' general aversion to that which has burned them in the past: When investors have lost substantial assets as a result of a poor investment, they become reluctant to buy the same investment again.

What, overall, does all of this have to do with a book that's counseling people to avoid individual shares in the first place? Much. For one, this book is not just about staying away from single stocks. It's also about avoiding the temptation to follow the rest of the crowd headlong into an investment because it happens to capture the public interest at any one given moment. Eventually decisions will have to be made by one or a married couple to shift assets from one investment class to another, or markets will start to undergo a series of stomach-churning dives or euphoric rebounds, and that's going to entice people to want to buy. They'll convince themselves that it's time to get back into getting individual shares, under the notion that perhaps you weren't all that ready to do this last time, or you've become smarter somehow.

Some will call this greed, but in reality, this isn't greed—it's just more fear masked as greed. It is fear that you will be "losing" by not winning, that you will fall behind others as the market goes off to the races. It's fear that you will miss out on opportunities in suddenly hot markets away from stocks, such as commodities or emerging markets—goaded by advertisers, financial experts, and cheerleading members of the media promoting this notion. But rallies can be participated in with much less risk than that of buying individual shares, at less of a cost, in a way that will salvage one's peace of mind.

Much of this may seem touchy-feely, but there's a good basis for understanding your emotions. But you need a few concrete ideas to help you get through the day without making decisions that deviate from your stated goals. Here are a few ideas, expressed very briefly:

1. Establish a level that will serve as the absolute low for a speculative investment you own. Obviously we're trying to limit trading costs, so you don't want to have it triggered too easily. A 15
   percent sell-off in a particular asset should be enough of a
   move to convince you that it's time to sell your holdings and
   move to a cashlike asset until the market rebounds.

2. Don't buy any investment product that hasn't been in existence
   for at least a year. Really, you need an even longer track record
   for an investment to be worth anything, but let's start with this
   much. (If we were buying individual shares, that would be one
   thing; but new products can quickly become oversaturated
   with investors having already driven prices to unsustainable
   levels. Or, they'll prove to be illiquid investments.)

3. Is the asset in question up 300 percent in the last year or some
   other unfathomable amount? Are you buying it because you
   believe everyone else is buying it and you're seeing it go
   straight up, like the Munder NetNet Fund? If the answer is
   yes, ignore it. Stay way far away. Don't tell me about all of the
   amazing gains you're missing out on—you've already missed
   the easiest gains, so don't bother now. The only prices that matter are where *you* buy it and where *you* sell it—not where it
   was when your neighbor bought it, etc.

4. Do you own some asset—be it a fund, emerging market ETF,
   or commodity—that has doubled in a year's time? Sell it,
   now—at least part of it. You'll feel better for having gotten
   some gains, and won't feel exposed if things take a bad turn. If
   it still goes up, that's fine—you still own it, and it's helping your
   portfolio still.

Those ideas aren't set in stone. They're kind of crude, to be perfectly honest, and may not come close to fitting your needs. But
there's a need to get comfortable with something other than inertia—the idea that you should sit tight just because things are going

well, or that you should hold on because of some perceived expectation that the market is going to rebound at some point. That's myopic, and in markets like what we've seen and what we're expected to see, potentially very dangerous. Just because you fail to make an active decision to buy or sell an individual holding in your portfolio does not mean you have not made a choice—you have made a choice, even if it is a passive one. To get truly secure with the idea that you're perfectly free to sell your holdings if you're not happy with them, it's going to take a bit more deconstruction of popular myths that have become pervasive in the last few decades. The primary tropes are the ones that say any investor can beat the market through buying individual stocks, and that the stock market, no matter what, is such a powerful force of good that it will eventually deliver the kind of strong returns that you are somehow entitled to even if you simply let it all ride.

As we shall see, this is not exactly the case.

Boiling It Down

- Beware of inertia. When you do nothing, you are making a choice—a passive choice. It may hurt more emotionally to sell an investment and watch it run higher, but it's worse to hold onto something as it goes into the tank.

- Be ready to sell assets that aren't performing. There's nothing heroic about holding onto losers. Forget about trying to break even.

- Have a sell discipline. Establish a level that will serve as the absolute low for a speculative investment, and if it falls through that, get rid of it.

- Don't buy any investment product that hasn't established a track record.

- Have you gotten a windfall from an investment that's gained something ridiculous like 300 percent in a year? Good. Sell it. Yes, you'll have to pay taxes. That's better than losing money.

- If you're considering a purchase of something that's up 300 percent that you don't own, stay away. Resist the temptation to follow the crowd.

Endnotes

[1] Author interview.

[2] Brad Barber, Terrance Odean, and Michal Strahilevitz, "Once Burned, Twice Shy: Naïve Learning, Counterfactuals, and the Repurchase of Stocks Previously Sold," Working Paper, March 2004.

[3] Author interview.

[4] Author interview.

[5] Terrance Odean, "Are Investors Reluctant to Realize their Losses?," *The Journal of Finance*, Vol. LIII, No. 5, October 1998.

[6] Author interview.

4

Investment Strategies That Turn Into Portfolio Nightmares

"Adventure. Excitement. A Jedi craves not these things."
Yoda, *The Empire Strikes Back*

There are some stocks that are going to outgain all comers—Apple Computer comes to mind; Google was certainly ruler of all it oversaw for years—but most of the returns that investors can generate now will come from effectively dividing up one's assets among different asset classes rather than worrying about individual names. Investors in recent years have generally been better off sticking to a broad investment strategy and eschewing individual stocks, which, by themselves, can do a variety of damage to portfolios.

The S&P 500 had a terrible year in 2008, losing 37 percent. But it is possible to construct a "nightmare portfolio" of some of the biggest, well-regarded stocks in the entire investing universe that would have made the S&P's losses that year look like a rounding error.

Names such as American International Group, the insurance giant that was brought low by exposure to derivatives; or the likes of Citigroup and Bank of America, supposedly safe institutions that borrowed a ton of money and used it to take big positions in poor-quality mortgage loans, or auto giant General Motors, which finally succumbed to heavy debt costs and the loss of competitive edge and was eventually restructured. The financial shares stand out as the most insidious investment of this period. There's no doubt that the banks were earning a mint during this period, but the delusion that arose was that risk had effectively been managed out of the market through the proliferation of complicated derivatives, mortgage-backed securities, and structured investments. These are notions to run from—the idea that fundamental dynamics that define investing have been repealed due to some sort of great invention that changes everything as we know it.

Perhaps it's unfair to pick out only the biggest, most obvious losers in 2008. But there were plenty of other stocks that were not forecast to take a walloping, but did so anyway. (We're making the assumption that most investors would have seen the problems at GM and Citigroup coming, but could not foresee the issues elsewhere. Investors are inherently convinced of the market's place as a forward-looking indicator, and yet the Dow Jones Industrial Average managed to reach a new all-time peak in October 2007, just two months before the official beginning of the lengthy 2008-2009 recession.[1])

But there was also the likes of aluminum giant Alcoa, which saw its share price fall to $6.23, lowest since 1988 as the economy fell off a cliff. One could even include General Electric, a massive conglomerate with its hands in everything from jet aircraft to financial advisory business to, of course, light bulbs. But that stock saw its credit rating slashed and was forced to cut its dividend amid terrible results in 2008; shares fell 56 percent that year.

In theory, beating the market is possible through effectively understanding when to buy certain sectors based on where in the economic cycle one happens to be, using certain measures of valuation, sentiment, and momentum to understand stock patterns, and through risk management that limits downside when one is taking big risks.

That all sounds nice. The reality is that professional investors have a difficult enough time divorcing themselves from their emotions not to want to chase popular investments for fear of being left behind. And markets can remain irrational long enough to convince nominally intelligent people to take risks that fall outside their stated investment parameters. Extended rallies in the market during periods where volatility indexes were calm (reflecting relatively benign and small daily movements in individual stocks and major stock averages) engendered a belief that investors could increase their risk without adverse consequences. And those who try to time the market, based on one's understanding of the economy, will find it to be quite the task.

That may sound trite, but sometimes trite makes right. Warren Buffett, chairman and CEO of diversified holding company Berkshire Hathaway Inc., and regarded as one of America's most prescient investors, said in his 2004 letter to his clients that it should have "been easy for investors to earn juicy returns" over the last 35 years by piggybacking on the success of corporate America. "An index fund that they never touched would have done the job," he wrote. "Instead, many investors have had experiences ranging from mediocre to disastrous."[2]

That's because for the most part they've been buying individual names. And popular literature aside, there are a lot of stocks that fail over time. The Center for Research in Securities Prices, which is run by the University of Chicago's School of Business, has more than 28,000 stocks in its extensive database going back to the beginning of the 20th century. Of those, just about 12,000 stocks are trading, and of those, only about 3,000 are really liquid, frequently traded names. Eric Crittenden, research director at hedge fund investment company BlackStar Funds, pointed out in a commentary that there are many more stocks that completely tank, losing almost all of their value, than people would expect. Crittenden looked back and found that between 1991 and 2008, the expectation was that 278 stocks would lose at least 75 percent of their value in one year. In reality, there have been more than 2,100, according to Crittenden. He believes that expectations for catastrophic losses are underestimated

because people exclude stocks that went bankrupt and took their listing off publicly traded exchanges. "This isn't in their database—all
the delisted bankrupt defunct stocks fall out of the database," he said.
"They look only at stocks that are currently traded today—that's
going to cause a certain amount of survivorship bias."

Why does that matter? Because it gives people the idea that
there's a floor on the losses of all but the absolute worst and leaves
people oblivious to the risks in lesser-known stocks. Many of the
stocks in question are fad-oriented, names that grow in popularity for
a short period of time before tumbling to the depths when it becomes
clear that they don't have the earnings or demand to justify their high
valuations.

But instead of using index funds and allocating funds in a disciplined fashion to various asset classes, many investors chase those
fads—when, as we shall see, early investors in industries that eventually changed the fabric of society often ended up poorer because of so
many failures in the early days of various companies in those
industries.

The "Experts" Fallacy

Many of you have probably at one point or another allocated
some of your money to funds that were expected to do well because
they were highly rated by fund ratings company Morningstar or
because of past results. But it doesn't take much for an investor to
destroy all of the previous gains he had worked to accumulate over
previous years.

The most famous example of this is probably Bill Miller, chief
investment officer at Baltimore-based Legg Mason, whose signature
fund, Legg Mason Value Trust, beat the S&P 500 for 15 consecutive
years, a record few can match. As the bull market wore on through the
1990s and the middle of the last decade, Miller's legend grew as he was

one of a few to stay ahead of the S&P 500 year-in and year-out. In that time, he built the kind of reputation that attracted more and more investors to his fund, which eventually peaked in size at about $20 billion in assets. In 2003, his 44 percent return crushed the S&P 500, ranking him in the top 1 percent of all large-cap blend funds for that year.

But the good times couldn't last forever. Miller suffered through middling years in 2004 and 2005, but he still stayed ahead of the S&P 500. In 2006, Miller's fund returned just 5.9 percent, and that year marked the second in a row that he trailed the average fund in his category, but this time, he failed to beat the S&P 500.

It got worse in 2007, when his 6.7 percent loss ranked him in the bottom 1 percent of all similar funds, according to Morningstar data. That year, the market managed a 5.5 percent gain, and Miller's style—contrarian value investing, as *Barron's* put it—proved horrific in a market dominated by rising inflation and strong economic growth. The environment in 2007 favored high-growth cyclical stocks such as the oil and gasoline names, as well as commodity-related shares. Those stocks soared, and Miller's holdings languished.

Everything came crashing down in 2008, however. The S&P 500 tanked in 2008, falling 37 percent, but Miller made those losses look like a safe haven. His fund plunged 55 percent, and the manager that had made all other managers look silly for more than a decade ended up ranking as one of the worst in his category over the previous ten years.

This slump was bad for long-term investors in the fund, as it becomes harder for someone later in life to make up for substantial losses in one's portfolio (for someone at the beginning of his investment horizon, a loss on a relatively small amount of assets can be recouped more easily). For newer investors enticed by Miller's track record, this was a disaster for them, too. It was at the peak of Miller's performance that the most assets were attracted by his fund—and those people who got in then, expecting big gains from a money manager who could put all others to shame, have been battered all over the place. But there are very few professionals who can consistently stay ahead of the market for an extended period of time who are also accessible by individuals.

In his book, *The Little Book of Common Sense Investing*, published in 2007, former Vanguard chairman John Bogle points out three funds that have been in existence since 1970 that have managed to outperform the S&P 500: Davis New York Venture, Fidelity Contrafund, and Franklin Mutual Shares. Because investing is a zero-sum game (that is, someone's 20 percent gain comes at the expense of someone else shouldering a big loss), there are bound to be a few winners. Still, it's notable that according to Morningstar data, at the end of 2009 Davis New York Venture sported a ten-year annualized return of just 0.84 percent (for investor returns, which factors in the drag on performance as a result of inflows, outflows, and taxes).

Bill Miller's five-year annualized performance of minus 5.9 percent (through March 2010) trailed the S&P by 7.8 percentage points—ranking him *last* among all funds included in Lipper's database of large-cap core funds. That's 664 funds. And this comes after the summer of 2009, when his fund (and many others) rode the wave of the market's 50 percent gains. For 2009 he managed a gain of 40.6 percent for the year, handily beating the S&P (which gained 26 percent), but the damage has been more than done. As of March 2010, his ten-year annualized performance was a loss of 2.7 percent, ranking him worse than all but 52 of the 387 funds that have survived that long in the Lipper category. Since 1982, when the fund was first started, it has an annualized gain of 12.13 percent, which is very strong—and if you were there at the beginning, you're probably still in good shape even as you've watched your investments get killed for the last few years. However, it's much less comfort for those who got into the fund in the good times and watched their money go into the sewer after years of outperforming.[3]

Many individual investors do the same as Mr. Miller in a quest to beat the averages. The litany of professional investors struggling to come out ahead of the market, and the reality that most fail to do this for more than a few years running, should be evidence enough for most individuals to reconsider what is a somewhat futile quest to outdo that which cannot be outdone without great pain. Yet regular folks who manage their own accounts tend to concentrate on their stock picks rather than on effective cost controls or risk management. The popular media and advertisements for the discount brokerages cater to this attitude that it's easy to figure it all out. The late 1990s were littered with commercials from the brokerages urging investors to get into the game, and lately those ads have made a roaring comeback.

This populist approach was appealing to investors amid a climate where they were being forced to depend more on their own resources to build a retirement nest egg. Social security had started to be viewed as the small, supplemental portion rather than a mainstay, and company pensions were receding as the favored retirement vehicle. With the 401(k) and individual retirement accounts becoming more important, investing became like home improvement—the province of do-it-yourselfers.

The difference is that investing is a bit higher on the curve in terms of knowledge needed than home improvement or landscaping. It's not quite on the level of medicine (one wouldn't operate on his own body), but it is more complex than simple house repairs (and after all, a plumber can always fix an overzealous handyman's mistakes). There's no do-over for retirement.

But for about two decades, investors weren't punished for excess, working through a long period of moderation where inflation cycles were short and downturns even shorter. Market gyrations were relatively safe to ride through, and that left investors who had until now little experience in the market with a sense of invincibility, one that's been punctured, time and again, in the last decade.

It's all just enough information to make people dangerous. Instead, one might ask, how can I spend my time figuring out proper asset allocation and understanding what my cost is? Jack Ablin, chief investment officer at Harris Bank in Chicago, and author of *Reading Minds and Markets*, says investors who already devote hours to trading have plenty of time to shift away from this to taking a more holistic approach. "You should take the time you would have done trading and apply it to this," he says. "Not only will you be able to make more consistent, more valuable decisions, you'll have some time left over," he said. Here, again, he credits the 24-hour, seven-day-a-week trading culture propagated in the media for the obsession with short-term movements in markets that dooms so many individuals. "Markets move a lot slower than people think and more deliberately...the markets news shows have to be on every minute of the trading day, and will often give investors a false sense of urgency."[4]

It isn't just the shows themselves; it's the advertising, which usually promotes whatever widget a particular company can offer that supposedly sets it apart from the rest, and focuses on the do-it-yourself-style empowerment principle. One such ad for E-Trade Financial that does this features a talking baby going on about his stock-picking prowess.

Another 2009 commercial for TD Ameritrade notes the charting capabilities available for individuals on its Web site, even though trusting charts, particularly in the absence of other information, is a rather perilous way to invest. Burton Malkiel, in his seminal *A Random Walk Down Wall Street*, has pretty harsh words for those who devote their time to chart patterns, because ultimately the charts will at some point fail to act in the preconceived pattern that is anticipated. This commercial features fresh-faced individuals noting things like, "look at that head-and-shoulders pattern!" in a ridiculously chipper voice, jabbering on about "pattern matching," as if finding such market patterns can be used as the basis for trading or investing, and if charts can't betray you down to your last dollar.

These advertisements don't point out how transaction costs will destroy most investors' attempts to beat the market over the long haul, but then again, they really don't concentrate on the idea that people should be saving for decades down the road anyway. They're primarily concerned with here and now, and anything that will entice you to do more trading, which boosts their revenue without making anything better for you. Charts and expected outcomes have a way of failing people; Long-Term Capital Management found that out in 1998 when the hedge fund brought the financial world to a standstill as a result of complicated bets that were designed to take advantage of movements in assets that ended up going the opposite from everything that was expected.

Steak Versus Meat Loaf

Without a doubt, endless repeating of bromides about diversification and cost containment would make for boring television. Sex sells, and stocks bouncing up or down are a sexier story than telling someone to save their pennies, invest in index funds, and be patient. (If winning the great game of buying and selling stocks is the sizzle, being patient isn't even the steak, it's dried-up meatloaf as far as marketing is concerned.)

This is why people would rather pick stocks, because there's an element of surprise to it. But popular financial business media makes this the centerpiece of its content, regardless of whether it is CNBC or Fox Business or various investing magazines. (Disclosure: I have appeared on Fox Business several times.)

Again, the best advice that one can get—saving money, diversification, paying attention to long-term goals—has an "eating your vegetables" quality to it, and it is understandable that financial media will not simply repeat the same advice, time and again. Yet the industry still remains caught up in the "stocks you should buy now" phenomena, with all of the razzle-dazzle associated with it. One of the primary reasons for this is the exclusivity factor. Everyone has heard the mantras about saving and being cautious; not everyone has heard that a particular IPO is going to soar through the roof when it starts to trade; not everyone has heard about a prominent analyst upgrading a company's outlook that will put a jolt into the shares; not everyone has heard that there's a load of bearish action on one company in the options market. Having access to these "secrets," so to speak, is exciting, and it fuels interest in company shares. Very few investing chat rooms survive long talking merely about diversification strategies, but message boards focused on particular stocks on popular Web sites such as Yahoo thrive, with rapid-fire commentary (most of it crude, uninformed, and grammatically speaking, an epic disaster) throughout the day.

For the three years I was the writer and editor of the *Wall Street Journal's* MarketBeat blog, I found the Web site got the most interest during the meltdown days of 2008. Readership spiked during the Bear Stearns blow-up in March 2008, and again during the entire August-to-December period of 2008 when Lehman Brothers went down, AIG became a ward of the state, and prominent financial institutions Washington Mutual and Countrywide Financial collapsed. The readership was often highest when writing about options-related activity in shares of those stocks, along with the perennial favorites, Google, Apple Computer, Research in Motion (the maker of the BlackBerry wireless device), Dendreon (a biotech company that was developing a prostate cancer treatment), Crocs Shoes (a favorite momentum play), and a few others. The volatile nature of these stocks kept interest high, and market enthusiasts still look to names of those types as trading opportunities. Citigroup, for instance, remains one of the most actively traded stocks on the New York Stock Exchange on a daily basis, and Google and Apple are usually among the daily leaders for volume on the Nasdaq Stock Market.

Several prominent investors interviewed for this book told of their appearances on CNBC and a desire to make broader points about market activity or approaches for retirement, but the channel gears itself towards whatever happens to be hot on a particular date. The channel might argue that it has changed its approach, but that's hard to believe when you see noontime anchor Tyler Mathisen teasing the next segment by noting that eBay had hit a new 52-week high and asking, "Should you buy it now?" CNBC is not alone among this kind of investing advice—magazines for time immemorial have been touting the next hot mutual fund and the stock to buy now, because repetitive pronouncements of the prudence of diversification wears thin rather quickly, and this does not sell many issues.

Nobody exemplifies the short-term trading mentality more than Jim Cramer, who is willing to ramble at length about a litany of companies that most have only a passing interest in. Oddly enough, the advice Cramer espouses in his 2005 book *Real Money: Sane Investing in an Insane World*, is relatively sound for the investor who shares a similar passion for investing as the manic former hedge fund manager. He suggests that people devote only a portion of their assets to speculation, while the rest probably should be invested in stable assets and low-cost vehicles like index funds. As far as buying stocks, Cramer suggested in that tome that the investor who wants to diversify should have positions in 10 to 15 stocks (ideally at least five), and should spend one hour a week doing homework on those names. So that's 10 to 15 hours a week. For some—like Cramer, who has an adrenalin level probably only matched by people running from hired killers—this is easy, and those who want to try to use diversification and a bit of speculating through purchases of single stocks should probably be reading that book rather than this one.

But many don't have that kind of time, and without it, it's impossible to get the kind of edge one needs to beat the market—something Cramer himself admits. "Investing can be a hobby, but trading can't," he wrote, noting that his wife, Karen, "is a fabulous trader," but "has failed miserably as a part-time trader." He says that those who cannot treat it as a job should look to professional management or some other way of investing their assets.

Furthermore, one essential truth that's been discovered by many a researcher is this: Professionals who devote their lives to the task have a hard time beating the market, and the average person tends to do even worse, particularly lousy at picking stocks. Those who trade more tend to compound their problems by layering in extra costs: In 2000, Berkeley professor Terrence Odean and U.C. Davis professor Brad Barber wrote a paper that examined trading costs among retail investors, looking at nearly 67,000 households with brokerage accounts, and found that the average household was outperforming between 1991 and 1996. They managed an annualized gross return of 18.7 percent compared with "an investment in a value-weighted index," which earns a mean return of 17.9 percent.[5] Not so bad, right? But once you factor in the overhead—the difference between bid/ask spreads, along with commissions—the trader's performance fell short, earning an average 16.4 percent annually.

That's not to say one should give up on investing altogether, or accept the idea of buying and holding and hoping things work out for the best. Many people did that in the last 20 years, and they ended up losing money at the point when they could least afford it. Others just made bad decisions at all the wrong times—the buy-and-hold investors who pay cursory attention to their portfolio run a greater risk at panicking at the wrong time. They're jarred awake to find the market is diving, they haven't examined their portfolio in months, and they sell shares amid a frenzy only to see bargain-hunters scoop up undervalued holdings that then go on to profit from strong rallies that follow.

Plausible Fads

One of the essential contradictions in investing is the desire we have for big returns and little risk. It's the thinking that drives the creation of, and demand for, products like mortgage-backed securities and complicated derivatives, assets that will supposedly be all things to all people. It's what drove so many people to blindly trust Bernard Madoff, because unlike other secretive managers, Madoff promised normalcy when all others promised the moon, and that (along with the exclusivity promised only to well-heeled, well-connected folk) drove the interest in his investments.

This applies to the stock market as well. Big dollars have been lost over time in short-lived fads, where a particular sector becomes over-valued on lofty expectations for something more than can be delivered. The last true fad was the 1996-1999 period, when Internet stocks proliferated due to cheap credit and on expectations that the invention itself would revolutionize various industries by increasing productivity and improving communication.

The thing is, the Internet did all of these things, and yet, most of the stocks devoted to online retail—business-to-consumer activities—disappeared. Networking companies and those that provided security software thrived, such as CheckPoint Software Technologies, but Webvan, Pets.com, Furniture.com, Kozmo.com, and others all went away. Some did well, such as Amazon.com.

There have been other fads grounded in even stranger ideas. Bowling stocks became popular in the 1950s when automatic pin-resetting machines became the standard, and investors became con-vinced that this diversion was set to become the country's biggest pastime. This did not work out so well. Solar energy stocks domi-nated the action among day-traders expecting an explosion in demand for photovoltaic tubes and other products designed to cap-ture the sun's rays. Those stocks soared between 2003 and 2007 before falling under the weight of unrealistic expectations in the lat-ter part of the last decade. There was a brief flurry of interest in stocks of vending-machine companies in the 1960s, while shares of movie theater companies also boomed for a while before dropping off the face of the earth around the same period of time. Such fads, particularly vending machines and bowling shares, are usually brief, and flame out quickly.

The more insidious manias, however, are those that either represent a rethink of the traditional role of a particular sector in the economy, or introduce a new technology that really does cause an alteration in the lives of people. Compared with a fad stock such as Crocs, maker of goofy looking shoes, the Internet is a much bigger, all-encompassing story that is easy to believe, and changed American life in a way that, say, bowling companies or the makers of Crocs shoes do not.

All at once, the market, being a discounter of future growth but also trafficking heavily in fears, wants, and hopes, overstates the case for the worth of a particular sector. To an outside observer, the Nasdaq Composite Index's ascent—it doubled between May 1999 and its peak in March 2000, just ten months—doesn't make any sense. To those participating in this historic boom in technology shares, it wasn't to be questioned, just enjoyed. A decade later, the index is still having trouble reaching half the value it enjoyed at its peak. Many of the bellwether shares of that fateful period have long since been absorbed into other companies.

Some of the memorable companies that sprang up during this period were a health Web site led by former attorney general C. Everett Koop, along with Pets.com, a pet-oriented retailer with a well-known mascot, a sock puppet. In retrospect, these companies were easy to understand—they were mostly e-retailers, selling goods in a particular niche over the Internet. That's a perfectly fine business model, but not one that was able to become profitable on a large-enough scale to satisfy investors in their stock. (One could see the steady demise of such names—a popular site called Kozmo.com offered to deliver just about everything to one's house, like movies and video games...eventually one had to start buying ice cream, and then the minimum delivery charge rose, and so on and so forth until the company died, victim of an unsustainable model.)

Some companies of this type thrived, obviously—Amazon.com exists to this day, and eBay is going strong as well. But Amazon was a rare case, and the stock languished for years before making a comeback about a decade after its pinnacle. eBay thrives mostly because it's the leader in what is essentially the world's biggest yard sale—and they're just a facilitator, not bothering to weigh themselves down with such overhead as inventory. Most disappeared; though many remember the sock puppet.

Many industries that have been woven into the fabric of our society went through severe growing pains, and with that they were accompanied by euphoric purchases of the next big thing among stock investors. Like the Internet, automobiles went through this. Car manufacturing boomed in the early part of the 20th century and for several decades later, but investing in anything but a few of the auto names did not provide the same kind of return as the market, according to a 2008 paper published by the Atlanta branch of the Federal Reserve.[6] For the period beginning in 1912 and continuing through 1928, $1 invested in a value-weighted index devised by Alfred Cowles would have returned $5.918. Cowles was an economist who put together indexes covering the early part of the 20th century, which has a dearth of reliable data on stocks.

A similar investment in the car companies in existence at the time, which include General Motors, Packard, Studebaker, and Pierce-Arrow, trailed the Cowles index. There were nearly two dozen auto stocks, and the average return of a $1 stock would have come out to $3.5504, trailing the market. According to the paper, similar patterns can be seen in history for railroad and telegraph companies, which saw a plethora of companies issue shares as the industry boomed, and quite a few run aground, eventually taken over by the few dominant players in the industry. This doesn't make the industry itself any less viable—just that only a few companies in the market were able to turn that into sustainable growth in the markets.

The more worrisome kind of fads, if they can be called that, is when well-regarded large-cap stocks or sectors start to dominate the equity market, and their value rises to a level considered incompatible with the growth potential of those companies. These manias are more terrifying, because they are based on a few semicoherent principles of investing. Well-known, generally strong investments are put on a pedestal, regarded as impervious to the whims of the market, so great is their dominance.

Things get even more perilous for investors who blindly put money into established companies (rather than new ones, which most understand is a speculative endeavor), anticipating few problems. Following the technology bubble, there were a group of shares that were thought to be impervious to the pain being experienced by most of the stocks in the market.

Even though many recognized the speculative nature of the market, some, such as Microsoft, semiconductor maker Intel, software giant Oracle, networking colossus Cisco Systems, and perhaps a few others, were considered those that couldn't go wrong. And without a doubt, those shares were better investments than many of the other names that experienced their heyday in the late 1990s.

But these four stocks—the Four Horsemen, as some referred to them—were drastically overvalued, and their performance reflected it as earnings sagged in the middle of the decade. After attaining peaks in 2000, the stocks have largely been what investors call "dead money," stocks that can't possibly justify their valuation and therefore trade sideways, or drift lower, for several years. Since the beginning of 2001, Microsoft has recovered, rising about 14 percent. However, Cisco is off by 41 percent, Oracle has lost more than 21 percent of its value, and Intel is down about 33 percent. In that time, the S&P 500 has given up about 18 percent, making only Microsoft an outperformer during that time period.[7]

Looking at a better buying opportunity—the market's trough in late 2002—produces more acceptable results for the other two names.

Between October 2002 and late April 2010, both Cisco and Oracle had more than doubled. Intel was a relative laggard, rising 66 percent, and Microsoft rose 41 percent, but that lagged the S&P 500's 46 percent gain. It's not as if all of these companies aren't sound businesses, earning tons of money, and providing employment to thousands. But their prowess earned them the unfortunate status as a stock where decisions didn't need to be made, other than to find a nice spot to tuck away one's share holdings until waking up for retirement in 20 or whatever-odd years. And if you've engaged in that strategy, vainly holding onto those stocks from the top of the market under the supposition that they would be bound to come back, you're still fighting an uphill battle.

This isn't the first time a group of specific stocks was anointed the status of Teflon investment. In the 1970s, there was another, larger group of names. They were called the "Nifty Fifty."

This share group was sort of the original list of "buy-and-hold" stocks. They were called "one-decision stocks" because investors were told they could buy the stocks and hang onto them forever. This was in the 1960s and in the early 1970s, and for a time, names such as Coca-Cola, IBM, and General Electric were justifiable as portfolio stalwarts.

To proponents of this strategy, these stocks were the kind of investments that would be money good for forever and a day simply because of their size and earnings prowess. This notion, of course, is ludicrous. Once stocks hit a certain level of valuation, and cannot justify their high prices, all that's left is the greater fool theory—that someone will always find the stock compelling at an even higher price. Really, that's what stock investing is—finding someone who will value your investment at something greater so you can sell it. When that fails to happen (and it can fail to happen for a number of years), you're sunk.

Well, things got messy in the mid-1970s during a period of substandard growth and rising inflation. The years between 1968 and 1982, when stocks were essentially flat, were good ones for active investors who knew when to capture the market's ups and downs.

Those who let it ride on stocks that were supposed to be safe were disappointed mightily. Not all of the Nifty Fifty were bad companies—Coke and IBM are clearly going strong today, employing tens of thousands of people and dominating their markets. But returns were elusive for some time.

Some companies, such as Xerox or Polaroid, started to have trouble, while others were discovered to not have been immune to the vagaries of the stock market. The Nifty Fifty was buoyed for some time by investor enthusiasm for these names, despite their lofty valuations, noted Jeff Fesenmaier and Gary Smith of Pomona College in Claremont, California.[8] Certain stocks were laughably overvalued, such as Avon, which traded at 65 times forward earnings expectations.

There is disagreement as to what stocks were definitely in the Nifty Fifty. There are several lists that existed during that particular time, and a list used by Jeremy Siegel, Wharton School of Business professor, does not match that of other lists. Fesenmaier and Smith note that the stocks in question were generally those that were overvalued by most conventional measures, yet were excused from typical valuation because of the long-term potential of these companies, and their place of importance in the U.S. economy.

There were lists maintained by brokerages Morgan Guaranty and Kidder Peabody, and the Pomona professors found that there were 24 stocks that appeared on both of these lists. All were accorded very high valuations during the early 1970s. "With the spectacular exception of Wal-Mart, the glamour stocks that were pushed to relatively high P/E ratios in the early 1970s did substantially worse than the market, in both the short and long run," they write. Wal-Mart Stores has posted strong returns over the next 37 years; in fact, from 1972 through 2001, just two other stocks posted a better annualized return, according to the University of Chicago's Center for Research in Security Prices; the others are SouthWest Airlines and Boothe Computer, later bought by Robert Half International.

Most of the others, even McDonald's, Walt Disney Co., or oil service giant Schlumberger, were pedestrian performers when compared with the S&P 500 over the next 20 years. (Some of the names are mind-boggling: Schlitz Brewing is in the group, for instance, along with fellow beer producer Anheuser-Busch. Sure, everyone drinks beer, and continues to drink beer, but until the entire country develops an alcohol problem, their market share is going to be limited, which is the kind of thing that should have been easy to spot.)

There's a common factor between these stocks and the recent run in the banking names, or even the telecommunications run-up in the late 1990s: All of these strategies have a veneer of plausibility behind their ridiculous valuations, and in that respect, it makes them more dangerous than the manias that surround oddball sectors or inventions that are new to the market. A lot of us recognized the silliness of some Internet ventures, but how do you tell someone that IBM is a bad investment? How do you suggest that Xerox, with its ubiquitous copy machines, is a poor investing idea? It's not speculative—at the time, it was a well-known brand that had a lot going for it, including steady earnings and name recognition. But that doesn't mean it was going to maintain a real value.

The Nifty Fifty were said to be able to justify their high value because the stocks in question were high-growth names and leaders in their respective industries. "The usual moral of the Nifty Fifty story is that investors became too enamored with growth stocks in the early 1970s and pushed the prices of their favorites to unjustified heights," the professors wrote. Sound familiar? The run-up in banking stocks in 2006-2007 was said to be justified because cheap credit and rising real-estate values would underpin earnings for those companies for years to come, and, after all, they were large companies that were leaders in their markets. Telecom companies, in the late 1990s, were thought deserving of their valuations because the entire world needed to be linked via cable or some other device. The early 1980s featured a strong run in oil and gasoline companies benefiting from the tight oil supplies that briefly boosted the price of crude oil to $100 a barrel.

But these strategies, eventually, were all brought low, or as a columnist in *Forbes* put it at one point, "People didn't stop buying the Nifty Fifty until every one of those stocks was taken out and shot."[9]

What's the lesson from all of this? It's that you cannot expect to garner strong returns because you're buying a stock that's considered beyond the pale in its long-term outlook. It's much too simple a philosophy, resting on the idea that stocks will always justify higher valuations because of anticipated growth, when even the safest of stocks can become overvalued and remain that way for a number of years, such as Pfizer did in the early part of the 2000s, or as Microsoft or Intel did around the same time, or JP Morgan Chase and the other banks in the latter part of the decade. Psychologically, it holds appeal because it promises outperformance but only with assets that are viewed as having an innate quality—but such investments don't exist. Stocks can be rewarding as an asset class, but they are not devoid of risk, and you should hesitate to invest in any area of the market—be it a sector or a group of companies anointed as market saviors—and consider it a substitute for buying the entire market, much less corporate debt, government bonds, or other safer assets.

Gone to the Dogs

There are other strategies that combine an investor's psychological desire for safety and predictability with the possibility of a "secret" way to beat the market. One of the best-known is the so-called "Dogs of the Dow," popularized in the 1980s by Michael O'Higgins, who runs O'Higgins Asset Management. This involves, at the beginning of each year, buying the ten stocks included in the Dow Jones Industrial Average that have the highest dividend yield, which is calculated by taking the stock's price and dividing it by the annual dividend. (A stock with a $30 price and a $3 dividend therefore has a 10 percent dividend yield, which is very high. Usually dividend yields are lower, anywhere from 2 to 5 percent.)

This strategy has worked in the past, particularly during a long bull market. That's because the stocks in the Dow that were priced lower than the other members of the index were sound companies, and likely to continue to pay their dividends even though investors on the whole believed they had less value than the growth stocks. Again, one comes back to the plausibility argument: These are well-regarded stocks, and this strategy depends on looking at this group of solid companies and betting on those that are said to be undervalued when compared with others—how could something like this go wrong?

But this strategy has not been in existence long enough for investors to know whether it truly stands up to the rigor of several market cycles. It cannot be denied that over a 70- or 100-year period, stocks outperform bonds more often than not. And maybe after that amount of time, the Dogs strategy will beat the market. However, the Dow Dogs are facing their first extended bear market after more than two decades of getting fat off a relatively steady market environment. And in recent years, it's been getting socked—illustrating how a couple of bad years of underperformance, particularly after an investor has been using the same strategy for years, can hurt one's portfolio.

In 2008, the Dogs of the Dow included Citigroup and General Motors, a pair of companies that had lost substantial value in the marketplace, and thus sported high dividend yields. The problem? Those companies cut their dividends to nothing and the stocks continued to get hammered. Citigroup lost 77 percent of its value in 2008; General Motors dropped 87 percent, and a few of the other Dow Dogs also weren't so good, leading to a 38.8 percent decline for the Dogs in 2008, worse than the Dow itself, which dropped 32 percent. (In 2008, just two of the Dow's 30 names ended the year higher—Wal-Mart and McDonald's, and neither were Dogs that year.)

Things didn't fare much better in 2009. The Dogs finished the year with a 16.9 percent average gain, while the Dow itself rose by 22.7 percent, and the S&P 500 did even better, so this strategy falls short.

So how does this affect long-term performance? It's not all that great. Headed into 2010, the three-year performance of the Dow Dogs is minus 6.6 percent, compared with a loss of 0.1 percent for the Dow. For the 15-year period ended December 31, 2009, Dogs had a return of 9 percent, compared with an 11 percent gain for the Dow industrials, a 10.4 percent return for the S&P, and a 10.3 percent return for Vanguard's Index 500 fund. Yes, 9 percent is good—but it falls short of what an investor could have garnered by buying the entire average, or by purchasing the Vanguard Index 500, which has a low expense ratio.[10]

O'Higgins, for his part, was undaunted, telling Beth Kowitt of *Fortune* magazine in January 2009 that there are "many years where you don't do well with it," but "those are generally the times when you should stay with it,"[11] because the strategy will turn around in the following years. Again, this may be true for an extended bull run, one that lasted through the middle of this decade, but an uncertain market such as this does not afford such comfort, and it exposes investors to the risk of underperformance, once again, if companies continue to struggle with dividends. It also advises passivity on the part of the investor: "Just leave everything alone and things will magically work out." And as we've seen, that's a loser of a strategy.

Historically, very few companies cut dividends. Between 2004 and 2007, Standard & Poor's Index Services reported between 29 and 32 cuts each year, compared with, on average, about 1,400 yearly increases. But 2008 was different, with 163 dividend cuts compared with 1,091 increases. Through September 2009, it was even-steven— 479 cuts, 479 increases.[12] Eventually, that ratio will probably snap back, and more dividends will be increased than decreased, but amid an ongoing bear market, where companies seek capital preservation, one cannot be sure that dividends will continue to rise automatically.

Furthermore, the Dow Jones members are not impervious to pain in coming years. (It's notable that one of the companies added when General Motors was mercifully eliminated from the Dow was Cisco Systems, the networking giant, which does not pay a dividend.)

The problem with strategies such as this is that they're eminently believable, and the fact that they don't rest on a speculative investment such as biotechnology shares or penny stocks nobody has heard of makes them sound safer to a long-term investor. But it still raises the question as to why anyone would bother using this as their way of getting an edge. These are well-known names; investors aren't discovering anything hiding under a rock, so the advantage of being early to a name just doesn't apply with well-established giants like GE. This really just leaves the idea of hope that a supposedly safe investment will yield upside surprises for an investor doing the barest of homework (really, investing in the Dogs doesn't involve any work—just looking at the chart from the previous year). It's shorthand for real work. And if it's shorthand you want, there are index funds: They won't outdo the market, but the only underperformance comes from one's own trading costs, and you can't kick yourself for trying a strategy that destroyed your portfolio when everyone else got rich off passive investing.

There are such things as safe investment strategies in the equity market. A portfolio of stocks picked from a pregenerated list is not one of them.

Boiling It Down

- Research shows that most investors, even professionals, are lousy stock pickers. Those who are good spend hours a day doing it. You're better off looking elsewhere.
- Be wary of fad investments that seem plausible—like those based around new industries that are having a big impact on the economy. Many investments in those industries will not pan out.
- Some investment strategies work only part of the time.
- Avoid the temptation to ride a herd into one investment, or a successful investor.

Endnotes

[1]National Bureau of Economic Research, Business Cycle Expansions and Contractions, http://www.nber.org/cycles.html.

[2]http://www.berkshirehathaway.com/letters/2004ltr.pdf.

[3]Data from Legg Mason Capital Management Web site, http://www.leggmason.com/individualinvestors/products/mutual%2Dfunds/annualized_performance.aspx.

[4]Author interview.

[5]Terrance Odean and Brad M. Barber, "Trading Is Hazardous to Your Wealth: The Common Stock Investment Performance of Individual Investors," *The Journal of Finance*, Vol. LV, No. 2, April 2000.

[6]Gerald P. Dwyer Jr. and Cora Barnhart, "Returns to Investors in Stocks in New Industries," September 2008, Working Paper Series, Federal Reserve Bank of Atlanta.

[7]Reuters.

[8]Jeff Fesenmaier and Gary Smith, "The Nifty-Fifty Re-Revisited," Pomona College, Claremont, California, http://www.economics.pomona.edu/GarySmith/Nifty50/Nifty50.html.

[9]Fesenmaier and Smith.

[10]Dogs of the Dow, www.Dogsofthedow.com.

[11]Beth Kowitt, "Dogs of the Dow for 2009," *Fortune*, January 28, 2009, http://money.cnn.com/2009/01/28/magazines/fortune/investing/investor_daily.fortune/index.htm.

[12]Standard & Poor's Index Services.

5

You Have More Options Than Just Sucking It Up and Accepting Losses

"The long run is a misleading guide to current affairs. In the long run we are all dead. Economists set themselves too easy, too useless a task if in tempestuous seasons they can only tell us that when the storm is past the ocean is flat again."
John Maynard Keynes, 1923

By now the peril of buying individual shares has been well-established. Now investors have another choice.

1. You can give up and not play the game at all, and withdraw all your funds from the market in favor of cash instruments such as money market funds.

2. Or, you can keep socking money into a 401(k) or retirement IRA, never check the statements, and hope it all works out without any active decisions on your part.

Both solutions are dangerous. Unfortunately much of what investors have learned is that one has to be "in it to win it," referring to being invested in stocks, so to speak. Anything else is assumed to be short-sighted.

The gestation of this notion comes, in part, from Dr. Jeremy Siegel, a professor at the Wharton School of Business. Siegel is known for his book *Stocks for the Long Run*, which suggests that stocks are the best investment, bar none, over the long haul. Various writers and analysts have already pointed out some of the flaws in his research. More often than not, he has been proven right, even if one restricts the data used to the years dating from 1926 to the present, which use the well-known Standard & Poor's 500 stock index, and ignoring the spotty records available back to the beginning of the 19th century. Dividend-paying stocks held for the long term are expected to be superior to bonds and all other investments. This hasn't been true all of the time, but it's not entirely incorrect.

I'm not here to argue for or against the work of Dr. Siegel—others have pointed out some of the inconsistencies in the older data, which relies on certain assumptions about dividends that may not be accurate. Regardless, it isn't so much the idea as it is the application of it, or rather, the misapplication of it. Well-researched, good ideas have a way of being perverted into something less than the sum of their parts. When Dr. Siegel published *Stocks for the Long Run* almost 14 years ago, he used historic figures to prove that stocks had long been the best long-term investment. That held true even as the U.S. became a more mature economy. But what is the long term? Five to ten years isn't, assuredly. Fifty or more years is a good definition of "long term," encompassing most of an investor's lifespan.

This book is not attempting to whitewash the reality that equities, over time, will eventually outperform the other common investment, bonds. But equities can be problematic over the short and even medium term. Short-term investors should probably stay away from equities in the first place, as you're talking about money that you'll need in two to five years. The question becomes less clear with a medium-term horizon, which can be defined at about 12 to 15 to 20 years.

But it is this idea—that dividend-paying stocks will outperform bonds and all other assets over the long term—that has changed into something more insidious as a result of a lengthy game of "telephone" that stretches from those who have read or are otherwise familiar with Dr. Siegel's work, to those who have not really read much of it, to their clients and viewers of CNBC, who think they get the idea of it, but really haven't heard much else. Instead of thinking stocks are the best investment over a long period of time, investors have substituted the bastardized idea that stocks are the best investment, all the time. And that includes those stocks that do not pay dividends, when stocks that do not pay dividends tend to do even worse than other stocks.

This unwavering belief in the market's prowess gained currency through the late 1990s and most of this decade as a result of the growth of what some could call "free-market fundamentalism," whereupon passive decisions by a "market" are viewed as superior to those made by an individual in all facets of society, but particularly in investing. Over that time, investors absorbed phrasing from the Wall Street lexicon—buying on the dips, stocks for the long haul—and substituted common aphorisms for judgment and an understanding of their own goals, the assets they own, and what they want out of their retirement. Who needs to answer such questions when you can simply buy stocks and hold them forever?

As a result, statistical analysis morphed into shorthand: Stocks were always the best investment. Investors were to hold stocks, regardless of what happened to their value over a period of years. Stocks were never to be sold, and in fact the only active decision one should consider making would be to buy more stocks when the market invariably fell. Proof of this can be found in the number of mentions of the phrase "buy and hold" in a Dow Jones Factiva search of magazine and newspaper articles dating to 1970. The phrase appears nearly 65,000 times! But the frequency of the phrase's use increases dramatically. In the 1980s, "buy and hold" appears in articles just 746 times. But in the "aughts," the phrase is referenced more than 55,000 times. One has to adjust to the possibility of greater duplication of articles as more media outlets are included in such a search, but it cannot be argued that this philosophy was drummed into the investor experience in the last decade.

The same can be said for "buy on the dips," the self-serving cliché that investors should look to stocks that have fallen from their heights and jump back in because they are undervalued. Again, this can be taken to ludicrous extremes. In the late 1990s, when I wrote for TheStreet.com, I conducted online chat sessions with investors eager for advice about the path of the markets. Because of TheStreet.com's rules prohibiting journalists from offering advice about individual shares, I was limited in what I could say about specific stocks. But I did at least make sure to tell investors asking about once-hot Internet stocks that had fallen to a fraction of their previous value that just because a stock's price has declined dramatically, that did not make it a value proposition.

Still, "buy on the dips" persisted. In the 1980s, the phrase appears in a Dow Jones Factiva search a total of 28 times, and many of those articles do not even reference the stock market. The notion exploded in the 1990s, and there are 771 mentions of this phrase in magazine and newspaper clippings, according to Factiva.

In the last decade, this philosophy, once the province of investment professionals using various metrics such as earnings multiples and earnings growth to determine the value of the stock, made its way into the mass market, and there are more than 1,000 mentions of this phrase in the 2000s. The decade begins with an article in the *Newark Star-Ledger*, dated January 5, 2000, noting the burgeoning sell-off in stocks (one that was set to turn into a 90 percent decline in the technology-heavy Nasdaq Composite Index), with this advice: "Don't panic and don't be swayed by big point moves up or down," counseling to "stick to your investment strategy, realizing that investments in stocks are generally *for the long run, from two to five years.*"[1]

Ugh. That quote is a perfect example of the distillation of everything investors and less-informed writers absorbed during the bull run—it's just enough information to suggest the writer learned something about investing, but what he learned was enough to misrepresent the idea of long-term strategy. Taking apart that statement, there's very little in terms of advice that's useful to an average investor.

Panicking, of course, is never advised, but a more alarmist perspective for the average person would have helped to get them out of the market in the early stages of the burst of the technology bubble. Even worse is the statement that suggests stock investments are generally for the long run, which the writer defines as "from two to five years." If the reader listened to this, there would be a catastrophe, of course. While statistics are on the side of those who claim stocks are the best investment for a multidecade period, stocks have often been the worst investment around for a vast number of two-year periods and plenty of five-year periods. Anyone trying to save money for an imminent purchase would have had better luck gambling it somewhere.

Conventional Wisdom? Yecch.

The last 20 years and particularly the last decade or so has been a time of what many called the "democratization" of the equity markets. But democracy, as politics shows, is messy and involves emotional decisions by a horde of people who sometimes don't have all the facts—what people absorb tends to run in the realm of cliché, or talking points, really.

Retail investors became attuned to these shorthand philosophies at the exact time it proved fatal: The nasty tech-led bear market of 2000-2003, and the even more harrowing experience in 2007-2008. Denise Shull, president of Trader Psyches, who studies the emotions behind investing, says that a good reason that people believe such mantras "is we believe in experts—particularly when we don't know a field. The market is very mysterious—because everyone forgets they are betting on other people—and so people are generally inclined to believe in conventional wisdom more than they would otherwise be."

For the most part, conventional wisdom stinks when evaluating individual purchases in the market. The popular phrase used to describe social and sexual behavior that sprung up in the 1960s, "if it feels good, do it," is deadly in the stock market. Usually, if it feels good in the stock market, avoid it at all costs. Rob Arnott of Research Affiliates puts it this way: "The markets don't reward comfort. They reward discomfort."

The essential meaning and usefulness of the "stocks for the long run" phrase had been lost, and instead investors responded in an even more damaging fashion. Schooled to believe they should hold their investments regardless of the situation, they, in a fit of stubbornness reminiscent of Pickett's Charge, gallantly stuck to their guns in the face of falling portfolio values—until that panicked, emotional moment when they attempted to achieve catharsis by selling all of their assets. This last moment, naturally, was probably the best buying opportunity for investors. Invariably, investors who nervously unloaded the losers from their portfolio at their lowest value probably later compounded this mistake by buying after said stocks rebounded substantially.

Human nature being what it is, people can only follow a discipline that's based on well-worn mantras for so long without some sort of documentable evidence. The phrases "buy and hold" and "buy on the dips" may be translatable into actionable intelligence when accompanied with charting technology, fundamental evaluation of companies or markets, and knowledge of economics, but by itself, it merely represents a combination of hope and expectations based on past experience. Eventually, that's not enough, not when an investor is staring at a 50 percent slump in her portfolio. Naturally, emotions finally take over—and the person in question sells at the worst possible time. You're not alone, as professionals do this too; financial advisors who are primarily charged with helping clients effectively allocate assets rather than pick stocks have not been shown to be any better at timing the market than anyone else. (And on top of that, they're charging a fee for their services, which means they're making the same bad decisions you're making and charging you money for it...where do we sign up?)

Where does such a panicked reaction come from? There are two culprits. The first factor is that investors, new to the market, strode into equities without much of a road map, and without having experienced the pain that accompanies a long period of poor performance in stocks. Just 19 percent of Americans owned stocks in 1983, down from 25 percent in 1970, according to the Federal Reserve's survey of consumer finances, reflecting a decline in popularity of investment clubs after a long period of lousy performance in the stock market.

By 1998, a total of 63 percent of Americans owned stocks, either directly or through mutual funds and retirement accounts. Those investors experienced years of low volatility and high returns—in fact, during that decade, the market went about seven years without once experiencing a 10 percent correction, according to researchers at Birinyi Associates in Westport, Connecticut.[2] That's an unprecedented level of stability, and it nearly repeated that trick after the lows of 2003, when markets went up, once again, in a steady, unwavering fashion until reaching its pinnacle in October 2007. Since investors were already using the rationale that the losses of the technology bubble were "deserved" because of the inherent ridiculousness of the Internet bubble, they didn't look at that as much more than a speed bump. With that kind of stability, everyone looks like a genius, and everyone is schooled in the belief that the market has an inherent grounding, when in times of turmoil it does not—thus leaving investors unprepared for when the market starts to go against them for an extended period of time.

The second factor—which stems from the first—is a lack of discipline, which comes from investors not having learned when the proper moment is for such reevaluation of one's assets and one's allocation. Having not ever learned the proper way to examine a portfolio, investors assume that their only recourse is to continue to hold their assets without any changes, even in the face of terrible portfolio performance. This is the equivalent of being told to "suck it up" by a tough-minded eighth-grade gym coach when you're doubled over in pain after running several laps.

But sucking it up is not an option. Not when it's your money. Sure, it would be ridiculous for investors to sell assets at the first sign of trouble; for one thing, it would be prohibitively expensive due to trading costs, and secondly, it would drive a person crazy trying to keep up with every move in the market. But research does show the benefit of some active involvement in one's portfolio, to the point of intervening and selling assets that have performed well, in addition to unloading those that have not done as well.

Here's the rub: It's hard to figure out when to sell, so the choice comes down to a person's own goals and a bit of understanding of what's happening in the market. This has turned out to be very difficult because the signs that exist when stocks have hit unsustainable levels are often ignored by investors who myopically believe markets will continue to sustain rallies.

For those who shrug this off and boldly suggest they can see the turns coming, consider this: The Dow Jones Industrial Average peaked at an all-time high on October 9, 2007, having surpassed the 14,000 level. That was two months before the official onset of the 2008-2009 recession, a time when investors theoretically should have been lightening up their portfolio, which is something very few were doing.

But most investors are unable to predict when sectors are going to turn. Professionals offset this by steadily pruning positions that they believe are going to fall out of favor in coming quarters due to changes in the economy, and add slowly to other positions that they believe will perform well as demand picks up or slows down. Again, this can all go wrong if bad bets are made—the aforementioned Bill Miller of Legg Mason bet on a rebound in financial markets that was not forthcoming and believed certain stocks were undervalued even though they had declined substantially. He saw his portfolio decimated as a result. And you face similar challenges in trying to determine when certain industries are going to do well and when others will not.

Still, this does not mean that individuals cannot apply certain levels of active management to their portfolio. Investors have the ability to alter the mix of their investments—be it from sector to sector, or from asset class to asset class—in their IRAs or 401(k) plans without much trouble. These accounts, rather than accounts that would be subject to taxes and other costs, are ripe for shifting allocations because they are protected from taxes until the money is withdrawn. Within that, investors can either elect to rebalance their portfolio (some companies offer automatic rebalancing to pull back on certain funds that have had outsized gains), and they can also shift their contributions to take advantage of a downturn. This is another one of Jim Cramer's ideas—figure out what your allocation to your 401(k) is going to be for the year (say, by looking at the allocation in your biweekly paycheck and multiplying by 26 to get the yearly contribution), and then bump up your allocation temporarily when markets experience severe downturns. This allows a person to buy certain investments at a cheaper price. Since 401(k) allocations can usually be altered as many times during the year as one wants, there are no additional costs, and investors are buying equities on the cheap as a result. In fact, the freedom afforded an investor in a 401(k) plan—which does carry some short-term costs—is perfect for rebalancing or shifting investments when troubles begin.

Unfortunately, most investors are terrible at figuring out when to get in and out of an investment, which is how the misapplication of the "stocks for the long run" mantra comes to bite them in the rear end. According to research from Birinyi Associates, the annual average return of the Standard & Poor's 500 index is 8.71 percent. But according to Birinyi, the average gain for weighted equity mutual funds since 1962—that's taking all actively managed mutual funds (not including index funds) and weighting the performance based on size of the fund, thus assigning more importance to the larger funds that continue to attract more assets—is a mere 1.18 percent.[3] It shows that the largest funds—those that have welcomed more funds from investors—have done worse than the market in general.

This points directly to the individual's inability to adequately assess what is and what is not overvalued—larger funds attract hot money as people try to chase performance, and as they get bigger, their performance suffers. It happened with Bill Miller's Legg Mason fund, it happened with the Munder NetNet Fund, and it happened with other popular funds from Janus, Invesco, and companies that produced a winning streak that enticed investors to flock to these asset managers. John Bogle, who pioneered the index fund through his Vanguard Funds, points out that smaller fund managers—those that limit their size to something less than $500 million—can beat the market consistently if they're adept enough at stock picking. Once they grow larger, they become a glorified, higher-cost index fund, and the costs of shifting positions becomes more prohibitive, eventually hurting returns just because of the sheer size of the fund. In addition, it's the investors who come in late—the ones who cause certain funds to be weighted more heavily than others—who feel the most pain.

For individual investors, what makes more sense is to start with index funds. It forms the core of the strategy I'm suggesting, because it starts at the point that you, the investor, can most easily control: costs. The lower your costs, the better your returns are after the attendant fees that come with investing, and the easier it is to come close to matching a benchmark (even though, as we'll discuss, that's not really the goal, either).

Other than a number of hedge fund managers, there were very few with a reputation for stock-picking prowess that outdid Bill Miller, and his downfall illustrates the peril of following someone based on reputation, on star rating, or most importantly, on past performance.

David Loeper, president and CEO of Virginia-based Financeware, an investment advisory, says that investors "can play the roulette wheel" if they like through the use of active management, but it opens up someone to the risk of underperforming the market, and badly, after years of gains.

Loeper runs separately managed accounts for his clients, and he, like many others, is a proponent of using index funds for various reasons: lower costs, more attention given to asset class management and the goals of a client's portfolio, but specifically points out that someone who invests in index funds or ETFs can only underperform by their fees, while someone who goes with active management runs the risk of falling far short while spending considerable costs to do so. With indexes, "there's no chance of over-performing, but there's value to not subjecting yourself to the risk of underperforming," Loeper says.[4]

"A young person who started in 1997 and spent 10 years straight outperforming by 100 basis points just needs to underperform by 3.2 percent, and he has then completely wiped out the advantage of outperforming for the decade," Loeper says.

In any investing environment, someone with a long-term horizon has to start somewhere, with a core portfolio of investments that are guaranteed to do as well as the market is doing. If you as an investor are not equipped—either with the time or the inclination—to buy individual stocks, and this book argues that for most, it is an impossibility, then one has to start with mutual funds or exchange-traded funds. With that in mind, index funds are the place to begin, but as we will see, they're not all alike—not even close.

By now one reading this book might conclude that your humble author is something of a pessimist, given to spouting clichés such as, "You can't fight City Hall," and the like, given the view that most individuals cannot, on their own, best the average return in the equity market.

It's true that some people indeed have shown prowess in constructing a portfolio that comes out ahead of everyone. Those are few, however—and it's not just individuals, it's the professionals as well.

Several researchers, in a paper financed by the Swiss Finance Institute, took a look at about 2,100 actively managed funds and how they did between 1975 and 2006.

They found that beating the market consistently is nearly impossible. Through 1990, about 9 percent of the funds were able to stay ahead of the game. But through 2006, the percentage of those that could consistently offer returns that outdid the major averages amounted to 0.6 percent, which is basically nothing.[5] Some of those that did beat the index also may have been getting lucky, which doesn't speak too well for the abilities of active managers.

This isn't entirely their fault. The study notes that about 1 in 10 were able to beat the market before expenses come into play, but that little bugaboo—the fact that managers aren't doing this for charity's sake—meant most of the rest of those that were actually outdoing the market were knocked out of the water once they paid themselves, their staffs, their research costs, their trading costs and other expenses. Overall, the researchers found that "the proportion of skilled fund managers has diminished rapidly over the past 20 years, while the proportion of unskilled fund managers has increased substantially."

There are a number of stated reasons for the decline in investment-picking abilities. One may be that mutual fund managers of 30 years ago are akin to hedge fund managers and strategic investors of today, according to James Bianco of Bianco Research. Past generations of mutual fund managers amassed larger positions in certain companies and used their ownership to force changes upon management, thus potentially improving the performance of a company. That's a role now left to private equity and other strategic investors— the Carl Icahns and Kirk Kerkorians of the world.

In addition, many mutual fund managers with real skill decamp to the hedge fund world, where they're free to run smaller, more nimble funds and charge big fees to do so, while the mutual fund they left suffers in comparison. And the increasing ownership of equities among investors has made the market more efficient: Fewer stocks, particularly large-cap stocks, are mispriced, leaving less opportunity for investment managers to take advantage of value opportunities (unless they dive deep into the pool of small-cap or micro-cap stocks that can potentially provide home-run returns).

The legendary investor Benjamin Graham wrote the seminal *Security Analysis* in 1934 with his partner David Dodd, and the book, and subsequent publications, became the gospel for value investors such as Warren Buffett. Through painstaking work, the book argued, one could find undervalued investments that were mispriced due to lack of exposure or understanding, and exploit that to beat the markets. But late in his life, he, too, came around to the "efficient market" hypothesis, which says that stocks are on the whole pricing all relevant information into their value. This is what he said in an interview in 1976 with the *Financial Analysts Journal*, shortly before he died:

> "I am no longer an advocate of elaborate techniques of security analysis in order to find superior value opportunities. This was a rewarding activity, say, 40 years ago, when our textbook 'Graham and Dodd' was first published; but the situation has changed a great deal since then. In the old days any well-trained security analyst could do a good professional job of selecting undervalued issues through detailed studies; but in the light of the enormous amount of research now being carried on, I doubt whether in most cases such extensive efforts will generate sufficiently superior selections to justify their cost."

These thoughts match what Charles D. Ellis, president of Greenwich Associates, said in an article called "The Loser's Game" in *The Financial Analysts Journal* in July/August 1975. He stated that "the investment management business is built upon a simple and basic belief: Professional managers can beat the market. That premise appears to be false."[6]

Index Funds: Not All Equal

As the Swiss Finance Institute pointed out, it seems as if the ability of managers to beat the market is getting worse, and part of that has to do with the saturation of information in the marketplace itself. Compared with the 1930s and 1940s, when a truly dedicated manager could separate himself from others through analysis and attention to all of his investments, the asymmetric advantage has all but disappeared, despite what the professionals in the brokerage and mutual fund industries would contend.

This brings us back to index funds. John Bogle, longtime head of Vanguard Funds, established the first true index fund in 1975, designed to track the performance of the S&P 500 index. The aim was simple: to provide the best performance at the lowest costs, referring to what he called "the great irony of investing"—that you "get precisely what you don't pay for. So if you pay for nothing, you get everything."[7]

He hasn't been wrong. Vanguard's Index 500 fund has mustered returns that have outpaced about 85 percent of the mutual funds in the last few decades. And that is, again, without doing anything but passive investing. That does not mean, however, that index funds are a monolith. There are nearly 200 index funds and exchange-traded funds tracking the S&P 500, and their performance does vary due to differing expenses underlying each of these funds. Some of the funds in question have surprisingly high expense ratios.

For instance, the Rydex S&P 500 "A" shares sport an expense ratio of 1.52 percent, according to Morningstar, the mutual fund research firm in Chicago. If it's pointless to pay a lot of money for a fund manager who is at least trying to beat the market, it's even more pointless to see returns eroded by a manager who isn't even trying! Returns are drastically impacted by this as a result. Over the last five years through November 13, 2009, the annualized five-year return of the S&P 500 is 0.48 percent. The iShares S&P 500 index, one of the more popular exchange-traded funds that mimics the S&P, has a return of 0.45 percent, so it's just a fraction behind the actual index, which makes logical sense.

The Vanguard 500 Index offerings come in several classes of shares; some of them, including the institutional shares, are actually outdoing the S&P by a few hundredths of a percentage point. The most well-known, though, the Vanguard 500 Index Investor Fund, established in 1976, has a total annualized five-year return of 0.40 percent. Naturally, it trails the S&P 500, but again, only by its costs.

The same can't be said for others. There are a number of index funds, including some that have been around for a couple of decades, which are providing no benefit to picking an index fund. Dreyfus's S&P 500 fund is up just 0.04 percent in the last five years; T. Rowe Price's Index fund has a return of 0.25 percent over the last five years, owing in part to an expense ratio of 0.35 percent, more than double that of Vanguard's 0.16 percent and more than triple that of Fidelity Spartan's ratio of just 0.10 percent.

These differences are not trivial. An investment of $10,000 in a fund that compounds at an 8 percent annual rate—optimistic, but let's go with it—will, after 35 years, be worth $147,853.44. Cut that down by half a percentage point to 7.5 percent, and that return drops to $125,688. And this isn't even complicated—it's not work at all to pick an index fund as it is to try to pick stocks. Losing money as a result of high expenses in a fund that's supposed to be doing just what the most popular market barometer is doing is downright foolish.

Some say an index that tracks the S&P 500 is the wrong way to go in the first place, despite the S&P's popularity as a market barometer. Burton Malkiel, author of *A Random Walk Down Wall Street*, argues that the transaction costs embedded in the cost of buying and selling issues that come in or leave the S&P 500 hurts returns. He suggests a broader index, such as the Wilshire 5000 or the Russell 3000, because those indexes cover a larger portion of the market. Because of this, the transaction costs are a bit lower, so the spread between the index's performance and the returns of index funds is smaller. Secondly, the best outperformance in stocks is often found in the smallest issues. The S&P 500 accounts for about 75 to 80 percent of the market's total capitalization, but it's that other 20 percent that provides the most opportunity for big rewards, he argues.[8]

This assertion, however, is somewhat belied by statistics. The Wilshire 5000 and Russell 3000's returns are on a par with the S&P 500 over the last two decades, so whatever difference comes from getting a benefit from having smaller companies in one's portfolio is eroded by the poor performance of other components. An investor, however, who truly wanted to overweight growth companies could buy indexes that track the Russell 2000 along with a Russell 3000 index fund—this then overweights small growth-oriented shares, again, also for a low cost.

Others argue that indexes that are weighted in favor of capitalization—that is, the index is more directly influenced by the biggest companies in the index—are part of the problem. The Standard & Poor's 500-stock index is a popular index, but a great percentage of the daily shift in the index is accounted for by several dozen of the largest stocks, such as Apple, Microsoft, Exxon Mobil, Wal-Mart and the other well-known names. Those investors argue that a "fundamental indexing" approach, one that is less sensitive to market capitalization and price, is a better approach. Rob Arnott of Research Affiliates has created a number of these indexes at his firm—they weigh stocks based on several criteria, including their underlying value, cash flow, sales, and dividends. How does this help? It avoids the problem of overweighting stocks that have run up dramatically and therefore become overrepresented in an index, like technology did at the end of 1990s and as financials did at the end of this past decade. "Each new day brings further empirical evidence that weighting securities by capitalization is the index fund's Achilles' heel," he wrote in a January commentary. Of course, that presents the challenge for investors on how to avoid that as well (other than hand-ing over money to Mr. Arnott, who, as smart as he may be, cannot manage the retirement funds of the entirety of the U.S. public). Investors can on some levels tackle this problem through equal-weighting of other types of indexes or ETFs of other asset classes or parts of the market, which we will discuss more later.

In addition, other asset classes are worthy of consideration, both in the U.S. and outside the U.S., that will help offset losses in other areas of one's portfolio with a modicum of effort. Foreign stocks are occupying a larger place in investors' portfolios in recent years for good reason, along with small stocks, long-term government bonds, short-term cashlike instruments such as Treasury bills and money market funds, and stocks invested in hard assets such as gold and oil, which tend not to react in the same way to the rest of the market.

So, what, then, can investors do to help offset their risk and pro-tect their portfolio from losses? The passivity argument helps keep costs low, but in a nowhere market, it's not all that useful, and you're going to need more from your investments as you should. There are a number of possibilities. Some of these are easy. Rebalancing on a yearly basis in one's 401(k) allocation is a snap—particularly for those who can do so automatically when they enroll in their plan. Establish-ing a level at which one should sell assets, such as ETFs or other investments, after a certain percentage loss is a bit more difficult, but there are strategies that attempt to go this way to keep losses minimal. (Anyone who immediately exited hot tech funds after it lost 15 per-cent of its value in 2000 saved themselves a lot of pain. The downside? When there are occurrences like the May 6, 2010 "flash crash," when popular stocks were suddenly traded briefly at a penny, a level that would have triggered sales for many investors.) Keeping a bit of money in Treasury securities that track rising inflation can help guard some of the portfolio against losses.

Other strategies, which will be discussed, involve putting a cap on the losses one will tolerate before shares in index funds or ETFs are sold and allocating funds among a number of different asset classes, more than you're used to doing in the past. Some of these ideas have their own pitfalls, and there are still plenty trying to come up with a better mousetrap that will solve everyone's problems with a simple formula. No such formula exists.

There are other ways to keep one's head up, avoid sticking it into the sand, while still avoiding panicked decisions, and a lot of this is learned behavior that comes from making mistakes.

More of this will be discussed in coming chapters, but first it's worth looking at diversification. We need to go through how seemingly diversified portfolios can get crushed in a market where assets all move together at the same time—and figure out what assets will truly hang tough when all sorts of stocks or commodities are falling at the same time. Getting this right will keep you from lying awake at nights worrying about your purchases or have you stressed out in front of the computer when you have other things to deal with, such as a job, a home, and a family.

Boiling It Down

- You don't have enough time to invest in individual stocks. Your time is better spent if you use it figuring out your diversification, what your goals are, and where your money should go.
- Stick with index funds instead of stocks. Start with the index funds that cover as much of the market as possible, because it decreases your weighting to the largest stocks—too much money allocated to big stocks sets you up for a fall if the market declines.
- Not all index funds are equal! Some of the best ones are the lowest-cost ones, because they're returning more of the market's returns to you rather than keeping it for themselves.
- You need to rebalance your investing assets at least once a year.

- Keep trading to a minimum in funds. Rebalancing at least once a year will be necessary, but the more you trade, the worse your performance due to transaction costs.
- Keep some money in safe Treasury securities.
- Don't sit back and accept losses out of fear of missing later gains.

Endnotes

[1] David Schwab, "What's an Investor To Do? Bulls Take a Beating," *Newark Star-Ledger*, January 5, 2000.

[2] Author interview.

[3] Birinyi Assoc., TickerSense blog, http://tickersense.typepad.com/ticker_sense/2009/11/mutual-fund-returns-dont-follow-the-heard.html.

[4] Author interview.

[5] Laurent Barras, Olivier Scaillet, and Russ Wermers, "False Discoveries in Mutual Fund Performance: Measuring Luck in Estimated Alphas," Swiss Finance Institute research paper series, No. 08-18.

[6] Bogle Financial Markets Research Center, http://www.vanguard.com/bogle_site/lib/sp19970401.html.

[7] John Bogle speech, May 15, 2006, http://www.vanguard.com/bogle_site/sp20060515.htm/.

[8] Burton Malkiel, *The Random Walk Guide to Investing: Ten Rules for Financial Success* (New York: W. W. Norton, 2003).

6

When Diversification Does Not Diversify

"It's not enough to say I'm going to be able to buy and hold simply because I'm diversified."
Mohamed El-Erian, chief executive at Pacific Investment Management Co., in June 2009

A few years back, 36-year-old Andy Vitus, an engineer working for a venture capital firm that invests in startup companies, was asked by his wife how much they could lose in a year, and he couldn't answer the question. After going over his portfolio, he realized something: What he thought was diversification was nothing of the kind—most of his holdings tended to mimic one another, thwarting his attempts at diversifying, which for years, has been considered the Holy Grail of investing. "Very few people have a good feeling for how much risk they're actually taking," he says. "At a first pass, a lot of portfolios, everything is just moving together. They've got ten different funds that would seem diversified but they're not diversified at all."[1]

It gave him an idea for a Web site that produces tables that show how correlated (that is, how strong a relationship) one asset has with another, which he called assetcorrelation.com. The site has certain limitations, as it mostly tracks the correlations certain exchange-traded funds have with one another rather than underlying futures, options, or bonds, but as a quick-and-dirty approach, it's a pretty good litmus test for an idea of how differentiated one's assets actually are. In many cases, according to Vitus, they're not all that well diversified, leaving them vulnerable.

"I see people entering whole portfolios in Qualcomm, Cisco, Microsoft, and Intel, and people seem to be taking a lot more risk for the return they're getting," he said. Vitus works at Scale Venture Partners, a San Francisco area fund that's "looking for the next Google," but acknowledges that many individual investors spend too much time doing the same thing—by buying a ton of technology stocks or other investments concentrated in particular industries, without properly holding funds in various other asset classes.

This may come as a surprise to some. The popular view is that even one with the most rudimentary background in investing—a layman among laymen—has absorbed the basic concept of diversification. That doesn't mean it's practiced, but certainly the concept is somewhat understood, the idea that one should avoid putting all their eggs into one basket. For those who grew up in a Depression-era household (or learned from those people), that may have been taken to an extreme. My grandfather, who grew up in the poor Weequahic section of Newark, used to spend his Saturdays driving from one bank to the next, looking to see who had the best rates on certificates of deposit, of which he always seemed to have one coming due. That CD, of course, was never to be reinvested in the same bank, nor would he open more than a couple of CDs at the same bank—usually three or more banks were involved in this process. He put a lot of mileage on his automobiles this way, of course.

Even with the demise of the one-stop-shop supermarket model of banks, shifting around from one financial institution to the next is something most investors do not have the patience for now. But they're aware enough to understand the need for assets in various places—that is, not just all in stocks, but other asset classes. Still, diversification has itself become more difficult in recent years: Stocks that were never expected to trade in tandem with other stocks now mimic each other, despite being different investments. Bonds, foreign exchange instruments, and emerging-markets stocks have all responded similarly to the global financial crisis. They have, over the past few years, traded in a similar fashion, and as a result it has canni-balized the benefit of spreading assets around in the first place—assets that were not supposed to go down at the same time now all go down at the same time.

But there are a few assets that are not tethered to others, and having a bit of each can at least mitigate some of the losses should the entire world go insane at one time. And more than likely, some of those assets that were meant to trade differently will do so once again.

All for One and One for All

Researcher Jim Bianco of Bianco Research in Chicago noted in 2009 that the correlation between the ten different industry sectors that make up the big S&P 500 had never been higher.

Correlation refers to the relationship between two variables during a period of time and is generally expressed in a range of one (perfect correlation) to negative-one (perfect inverse correlation), though it can also be expressed in percentage terms. The most basic example of correlation would be two kids on a seesaw—as one goes up, the other goes down, for a perfect inverse correlation.

In the markets, there are very few examples of perfect correlation, either one way or another—most assets, at one time, move independently of others, at least to some extent. Within the Standard & Poor's 500 stock index, there are ten industry groups, as follows:

- Consumer Staples (things you need, like toothpaste)
- Consumer Discretionary (non-necessities)
- Energy (oil and gas producers)
- Financials (banks, mortgage companies, insurance)
- Health Care (insurers, pharma companies, hospitals)
- Information Technology (computers, chip makers)

- Industrials (equipment companies, construction)
- Materials (timber, steel, rubber)
- Telecommunications (cell phone makers, AT&T)
- Utilities (Uh, utilities)

Looking at the S&P 500's ten industry groups, what's striking over the six-month period ending January 2009 is that these sectors were all matching each other, move for move. The sector that has been least correlated—that is, showing the lowest level of commonality in movement with the overall index—is the telecommunications index, with a positive correlation of a staggering 91.6 percent.[2] The other nine sectors all have a higher correlation, suggesting that they're moving together nearly in lockstep, particularly industrial stocks such as General Electric and Caterpillar, which as of January 2009 had a 99.7 percent correlation with the overall index on a rolling six-month basis.

Bianco blames this on the Federal Reserve's perpetuation of a boom-bust cycle. It begins with a period of strong economic growth underpinned by low interest rates—such as the 1996-2000 era—when the easy availability of credit makes various assets more attractive. The cycle busts with the introduction of higher rates, and most of the market slumps (2002-2003).

What happened in the next few years was more striking. The Federal Reserve, in the wake of the September 11, 2001, attacks on the U.S., and the subsequent recession (a minor one by most measures), dropped interest rates to exceedingly low levels and maintained those low interest rates for several years. Investors had been somewhat scared out of stocks for a time after the bursting of the technology bubble, so the next bubble formed in real estate. Eventually, though, stocks ascended to previous heights and went beyond, as capital found its way into various markets. This cycle lasted through October of 2007, when the stock market hit a peak, just a couple of months before the onset of the worst recession the country has seen in at least a quarter-century, if not in the post-World War II era.

What results is a cycle where credit is flowing like a fire hydrant gushing water into the streets in downtown Brooklyn, followed by one where lenders fold up their tents, lock down their storm doors, and wait for the tornadoes to pass. In such situations, one gets pretty undifferentiated results—the entire market goes up, and then the entire market goes down.

As stated, a new and innovative name, like Google, will outpace the rest—Google more than quadrupled between the beginning of 2005 and November 2009, a time period when the S&P 500 was flat—but much of the market basically acted as one for these periods. Because of the imbalances that exist in the economy, the Fed is likely to continue to facilitate easy credit for a number of years, which will continue to support markets, more or less indiscriminately (save for companies that are truly struggling). One year after the market finally bottomed out in March 2009, major averages had managed a gain of about 70 percent, and the Federal Reserve had only started to remove the extraordinarily accommodative policies it had put in place as a result of the recession. The threat of inflation once the economy eases to a more normal path makes another round of sharply tightened standards further down the road another possibility, and it's not difficult to believe the stock market will take things hard when that happens—the imbalances are that great. "We're not making any forward progress with the market right now," Bianco said. "Since it is largely driven by cheap money or expensive money, that's why you get all the markets to rise together or fall together."[3]

Individual investors only compound the problem by concentrating their portfolios in equities with a bit of fixed income. Investors put 70 or 80 percent of their portfolio in mutual funds, and then they buy investments that tend to mimic one another, particularly in their retirement accounts. If you look at your statement, you probably have a dedicated S&P index fund, and you've paired that with a growth fund and a value fund, and maybe a bit of small-cap (which is likely going to mimic the growth fund), and leave about 5 to 10 percent for international stocks and another small amount for the bond market. Voila! The diversification that you sought has not been achieved— instead, you have ended up with what hedge fund manager Ali Sanghvi of New York calls "fake diversification."[4] What's that mean? You own a lot of different things, but they're all pretty much the same, and it's not much comfort if the market loses 20 percent in a year if your investments lose 15, 19, 22, and 25 percent.

Professionals, too, can fall into this trap, but in a different way. Once a manager owns 40 to 50 stocks or more, their investments are starting to trade similarly. So if you own several funds—some of which own the same stocks—what you have is one large behemoth, instead of a few investments that offset each other, and it's a costly hydra-headed beast instead of an equity portfolio concentrated around a low-cost index fund.

The problem, investment managers say, is that people are some- times guilty of overdiversifying, buying too many different funds for their investment portfolio without considering the similarities between certain investments. Mid-cap and small-cap funds, particu- larly the broad ones, are very similar; small-caps are a bit more risky, but both types of assets tend to act similarly in various markets. Broad-based growth funds don't need to be purchased next to broad index funds; a person should only own so many different international funds. "We're taking on new clients, and almost everyone who comes into our firm has five or six funds that are all closet S&P 500 funds," said David Marotta, president of Marotta Wealth Management in Charlottesville, Virginia, also an advocate of indexing.[5]

Sectors: Slicing Up the Pie

Buying individual shares is a perilous road. But at the same time, you know you're going to have to do more than simply throw a bunch of money into an index fund and let it all ride until the day you come home from your job with a gold watch signifying the end of your working life.

Sector allocation would seem to be a middle ground here. We've already discussed how certain sectors are generally thought of as better purchases in certain economic environments, while others are better for others.

The consumer discretionary stocks, technology, industrials, and financials are considered the prime targets for investment during expansions. Consumer staples, utilities, and health care are generally better suited for recessionary periods, with telecommunications also in that group. Energy stocks are more for expansions, and the same goes for materials. That's the conventional wisdom, anyway.

The accepted notion has been that one has to shift from certain sectors to other sectors to outperform the market. What's interesting is this is one area where the amount of study has been pretty limited, and those who have looked at it have found that idea wanting. Plenty of academics have looked at the shifting sands of individual shares, and industry-level rotation is one that has been studied often. But sector rotation efforts have been touched on in a few important studies and so far, they're inconclusive. The basic upshot is that sector rotation can have a positive effect on one's portfolio when taken in a vacuum—but long-run historical data presents a more mixed picture, and of course, once transaction costs and taxes come into play, returns are again much less favorable for individuals. Mostly, it shows that sector rotation strategies can be a winning way for investors in the market, and as Jack Ablin, chief investment officer at Harris Bank points out, it puts you in the position of making fewer decisions. "If you're an investor spending your time gathering stories on individual stocks you're already allocating a lot to this pursuit anyway," he notes, and with the proliferation of sector-based ETFs and moreover, industry-based ETFs that look specifically at a subset of a sector, such as water companies, or Internet names, or gold and silver miners, or insurance companies, puts you in the position of designing portfolios with appropriate sector weightings without betting on one individual name in the sector itself.

It's getting boring to say this by now, but I'll say it again—most of this stuff works only if you're brilliant enough to recognize when the economy is shifting from early expansion to a later expansion, and then from late expansion into a recession, and then back again. Many professional investors advocate complicated approaches that suggest shifting away into certain kinds of assets in the early part of an expansion and others later, and still different ones in a recession, both early in the recession and late in the recession, when people start to look forward to the recovery in demand.

For instance, if it's well-known that the economy is worsening, discretionary purchases take a backseat as you and most others decide to pull back and save a little money. On the margin, that's meaningless, but when tons of people make that same decision, suddenly the receipts at Coach or Nordstrom's are going to look a little thin, and then the shares don't look as well-valued anymore. Other kinds of companies reduce hiring and capital investment, and so the heavy machinery companies like Caterpillar and Deere & Co. find their demand sapped. This happens more slowly, but it happens. It also explains why sectors such as utilities and consumer staples stocks outperform—people tend to like to keep their lights on and the heat running, and they're not going to give up on toothpaste or toilet paper in any situation short of an apocalyptic one. It also makes it understandable why investors, on an asset class level, would want to retreat to the safety of government debt and other types of high-rated debt over more risky assets.

Timing the market (and really, what is sector rotation but a bald-faced attempt to time the market) is not easy under any circumstance. So you could be told to try to move away from utilities and food companies while the economy is getting stronger, and stay away from industrials and growth stocks when demand is sagging.

Certainly, there are many who see this as possible. Professional managers move from sector to sector by purchasing and selling individual shares. But sector funds continue to grow in popularity as well. Fund management giant Fidelity Investments offers more than 40 such funds.

The pros use such funds a lot too, and those trying to keep costs down take advantage of the expanding market in exchange-traded funds, which trade like stocks, and are designed to mimic the performance of a particular index, be it for a sector, market cap size, particular country, or investing philosophy (value or growth). There are more than 225 sector-specific exchange-traded funds on the New York Stock Exchange currently, and that list continues to grow.[6] If one is good enough at this, you can do well—but once again, it requires perfect timing, not just decent timing.

The problem is that we generally have a hard time understanding when these inflection points are about to hit, and as a result, we miss those points when rotation from one sector to another would have a positive impact on our holdings.

Most of the time, investors go the other way. They treat sectors the same way they treat individual shares—overinvesting in one sector instead of spreading out the risk; holding onto those stocks even though they're sitting on ugly losses; and following performance by jumping into popular sectors just as they've become most overvalued. Interest in technology shares was at its height at the end of the 20th century. For the entire 1990s, the S&P's information technology did not have one year where returns were negative, holding the longest streak among the ten sectors. Things kicked up in the second half of the decade, with returns of nearly 39 percent, 43 percent, and 28 percent in 1995, 1996, and 1997. And then tech really went bananas, gaining 78 percent in consecutive years, in 1998 and 1999.[7] The number of technology funds grew exponentially, and money flooded into the sector. This was the time period when fund managers and registered investment advisors frequently confided in me, letting me know that they had started to lose clients for *not chasing the market aggressively enough*. These were the days when popular magazines started to ask whether the Warren Buffett approach—finding a good company at a reasonable valuation and holding it forever—was dead, in part because Buffett's purchases did not frequently rally by 50 to 80 percent in a single year. And it's also when share turnover really started to kick into high gear. The New York Stock Exchange reports yearly turnover statistics on its Web site. For decades, yearly turnover was between 10 and 20 percent, so one-tenth to one-fifth of a firm's market value changed hands during the course of a year. As the 1980s began, that ticked up into the 50 to 60 percent range, but by the time the technology bubble really got going, the market was seeing average annual turnover rates of 80 percent, suggesting that most of a firm's shares were being traded during the year.[8] Now, turnover rates easily exceed 100 percent, so investors really aren't holding stocks all that long anymore, because they're convinced that more frequent trading of shares and shifting from one sector to the next will help them outperform others. It hasn't worked; the herds of people moving from one sector to another are often chasing performance, and they're adding in tons of fees for trading as well.

Invariably, like individual shares, stock sectors become oversaturated with new investors, and after an industrywide decline in revenue and a collapse in earnings, they get tattooed as investors rush to the exits. At the end of 1999, the technology sector accounted for 29 percent of the S&P 500. Then the collapse came, and the tech sector was hammered in 2000, 2001, and 2002. By the end of 2002, the sector was just 14 percent of the S&P. It's not the only sector to have undergone a severe revaluation in this manner. Financial shares were strong performers through most of the decade before killing portfolios in 2007 and 2008.

Three professors at Massey University in New Zealand, looking back at stock market data to 1948, found that "different sectors do not significantly and systematically outperform other sectors and industries over the business cycle in the way conventional market wisdom would like us to believe happens."[9] They looked at the markets from 1948 through 2006, and took a look at sector rotation strategies for five stages of the economy—early, middle, and late expansion, and early and late parts of recession.

"If it is indeed the business cycle driving outperformance an investor who can perfectly anticipate business cycle stages and rotates sectors using conventional wisdom should generate the highest risk corrected outperformance," the Massey University trio notes. The problem is the margin for error is slim: Those who timed cycles perfectly beginning in 1948 through 2006 were able to outperform by 2.3 percentage points. That performance slips pretty quickly if you're not dead-on accurate with when to get in and out of sectors. If you anticipate a turning point one month in advance, the margin falls to 1.9 percent, and to 1 percent if you're two months early. And once again, this doesn't even include the costs of trading, which will be sizable, along with taxes and any other fees.

Conversely, being one and two months late reduces outperformance to 2.2 percent and 1.8 percent, respectively, and again, this is only if you time it exactly right. "We do not exclude the possibility that there are practitioners who profit from sector rotation," they say, cautioning that "the outperformance of these investors has little to do with what practitioners claim is the main driver of sector rotation outperformance: systemic variation in sector returns across the business cycle."

Analysts blogging on the CXO Advisory Web site also found this to be true. They took a look at the nine sector exchange-traded funds offered by State Street Global Advisors that match portions of the Standard & Poor's 500 stock index going back to 1998 to see if any of them showed tendencies that would mark them as better, more forward-looking indicators, or as market laggards. They found precisely nothing—the sectors are so closely correlated with the market overall that their predictive power was almost nonexistent.[10] The sectors least correlated with the overall market—energy, consumer staples, and utilities—showed very little. (Utilities, as it turns out, lag the rest of the market, so they have defensive characteristics.)

The professors note that *Business Week* in 2002 suggests that "if you are in the right sector at the right time, you can make a lot of money very fast," as if that's an easy trick. Obviously, if that statement is true, the opposing must also be true—if you're in the wrong sector at the wrong time, you can lose a lot of money very fast, but the article does not mention this. The Massey University trio say being in the right sector at the right time is rather difficult, making it unlikely that an "investor/trader can outperform the broad stock market using a sector rotation strategy. Moreover, an arguably easier-to-time flight to cash during the first half of recessions offers greater potential."

Again, the problem with this approach is that for many years there has been a lot of accepted wisdom about shifting from one sector to another and very little study on what to use as the turning points in question. Much orthodoxy exists in the marketplace as to how one sector is sure to beat another sector at a considered point in time. Plenty of well-known investors appear on television to utter bromides about "having to be in technology now" or how "the stock market never recovers without the financials" or "you've just got to be in those deep cyclical stocks at this stage of the game." Jim Cramer, in his 2005 book, put together a large chart on when to buy and sell such sectors, and Standard & Poor's published an entire book on this strategy in the mid-1990s. Those who do put this advice down on paper use a number of different complicated approaches. Jack Ablin, who runs investment strategy at Chicago-based Harris Bank, runs screens that look at sectors through the prism of valuation, the economic backdrop, the slope of the Treasury yield curve, investor psychology, and momentum. That's a pretty well-defined set of characteristics, but it's also painstaking, and even he admits it near the end of his

Reading Minds and Markets, writing, "By this point, your head is probably spinning." Indeed.

With this in mind, another group of professors set out to figure out if a simpler approach can be arrived at, and in some way, they did end up finding it. In a paper published in June 2007, several researchers did find that there's some value in a sector rotation strategy—one that bases its signals off the Federal Reserve. "An easily identifiable signal of Fed monetary policy could have been used to successfully guide a sector rotation strategy in the U.S. equity markets," they write, after having looked at the 1973-2005 period.[11]

What's the upshot? An improvement in returns of 3.4 percent per year over the benchmark, and the best period of performance comes in the years when returns are leaner. Unlike others trying to call the tops and bottoms of expansions, these four researchers instead tried to stick to as little movement in the portfolio as possible, pegging their shifts to changes in the Federal Reserve's monetary policy. "Trading costs would be relatively low versus strategies that are based on indicators such as the inflation rate, the default premium, the dividend yield, or the market P/E," they write.

The approach is a simple one: They put equal weight on the six more cyclical sectors of the economy (cyclical consumer goods, cyclical services, general industrials, information technology, financials and basic industries) at times when monetary policy is considered expansive. When the Fed is tightening rates, however, they sell those stocks and put equal weight on the noncyclical sectors of consumer goods, services, utilities, and resources. It's this latter period where the money is made. During a period of time when the Fed is maintaining low rates or cutting rates, a market rotation strategy returns 20.26 percent annually, while investing in the benchmark yields a 17.98 percent return. But during restrictive periods, the rotation strategy returns 10.23 percent, while following the benchmark returns just 5.32 percent.

What's significant about this study in particular is that it does manage to identify a way in which investors can aim to shift their allocation based on an easily defined marker—changes in the Federal Reserve's discount rate. They acknowledge that identifying the point when you're supposed to rouse yourself from your slumber and shake up your portfolio isn't easy, but it's at that point when there's the most benefit. And even though just about every "introductory investments textbook" talks up the idea of investing in cyclical stocks during upswings and less cyclical ones during recessions, few have put forth a simple way to put this into practice—and they hope their example does the trick. Of course, professional investors are going to take more time and add together more variables, as Jack Ablin and many others do already.

The enticing possibility of ways to stay ahead of the market—or at least offset some of the extremes your portfolio will undergo if you stick to passive indexing—should be intriguing. It's important to note that the sectors Conover et al. are referencing are very generic in their identifications—resource shares, industrial shares, finance—and don't get more specific than that. And that's because industries change over time; the industrial industries were dominated for a time by railroads and later automotive companies; the go-go names in technology were once computer manufacturers, and later chip companies, followed by networking and Internet names. Certain types of consumer goods have fallen out of favor while others have become more prominent. When growth patterns change and industries mature, they become less loved by growth investors and undergo a period of transformation as other buyers step into the mix. But sometimes certain companies dominate a sector—such as the pharmaceutical companies did in health care—so completely that we start to mistake their growth for the entire sector's growth, and relying on that to carry you through for years on end is a mistake.

The health care sector was one of the strongest performers during the 1990s. This sector of the S&P, led by pharma giants Pfizer,

Merck, Johnson & Johnson, and Schering-Plough posted double-digit returns for five consecutive years, from 1994 to 1998, and in three of those years returns surpassed 40 percent. Health care stocks haven't been the same since. The major pharmaceutical names peaked in terms of market value around the end of the decade. What followed was two years of negative returns, one solid year (13 percent in 2003), four more years of blah returns, and then the disastrous 2008, in which health care's 25 percent drop was actually better than the average for the rest of the market.[12] The pharma giants, once darlings of the growth crowd, have been dragging their feet ever since. This type of performance leads David Marotta to point out that you shouldn't rebalance into specific industries.

"If 100 years ago you were invested 80 percent in buggy whips and 20 percent in this new technology called automobiles, well, one was doomed and the other was not," he said. "Sectors in the economy change and they're meant to change and the ones that are dwindling are not going to come back. Rebalancing back into things like airlines or manufacturing almost never works."

Some of health care's underperformance, then, is a result of a shift in earnings away from the large pharmaceutical companies as they struggled to cope with the emergence of generic alternatives to popular drugs, and also the lack of a pipeline to replace those drugs. They're not the only sector that has succumbed to chronic underperformance after a period of crazy growth. The tech sector's run is well-chronicled. But the energy sector also stands out for its spectacular run from 2003 to 2007, when it rose at least 22 percent in every year. It was down 36 percent in 2008, and only gained 5.7 percent in 2009, but it's hard to believe the sector can continue this kind of run with commodity prices likely to slip in coming years and global demand unlikely to be sustained at levels seen during the boom periods for major emerging markets through the last decade.

Subsectors are also ripe for speculation, as we tend to get caught up in the idea of life-changing inventions. There are plenty of people out there betting on the ascendance of new industries focused on clean technology, solar power, alternative energies, new infrastructure, and clean water development. Some of these will work out as investments in the stock market and others will not. If it's worth it to you to try to capture these ideas, invest in all of them and make it a part of your larger portfolio; this way, the exposure is there without making targeted bets.

The shift between sectors in some ways is a bit academic now because of the tightening in correlation between the different industries in the market and the overall average. It may be that this is a bit too granular—and if that's the case, most of your homework will be based around effectively dividing up your assets into stocks, bonds, cash, commodities, and a few other classes, areas of the market that definitely trade differently than the rest of the market. Investors often believe they're diversified as a result of owning stocks in two or three industries. But they're not, and sector plays are so much noise without a larger plan on what to buy and sell.

When Value Is Growth and Growth Is Value

Why do mutual funds act similarly even though they're ostensibly different kinds of funds? One of the primary reasons is that they own the same underlying assets! For example, more than 2,500 investment managers, including mutual funds and hedge funds, own shares of General Electric, the diversified conglomerate that has its hands in various parts of the economy. Of those, 58 are index funds—which should be obvious. They account for 16 percent of the shares held.[13] The next category of fund managers is what famed manager Peter Lynch termed "GARP," or "growth at a reasonable price." There are more than 450 funds defined as such that own GE, and they have $14 billion in positions in GE.

But the two fund groupings that come next? Core growth...and core value! The two fund strategies couldn't be more different. Managers running a core value fund are focused on buying companies with a low valuation in relation to the market or similar companies. They tend to have P/E ratios below the rest of the S&P 500, and a low growth rate.

Core growth funds, on the other hand, are buying blue-chip names that tend to be among the best in terms of earnings and revenue growth—and attract, as a result, *bigger-than-expected* P/E ratios. Somehow, General Electric simultaneously qualifies as both.

This phenomena isn't limited to GE, which can reasonably be considered something to everyone, as diversified as it is. Core growth funds have about $31 billion, combined, in shares of Exxon Mobil—while core value funds have about $23 billion. Pick almost any large, well-known stock, and value and growth funds are all over it, even those that should ostensibly belong to one group and not the other. Shares of First Solar, a high-flying solar panel company that gained a ridiculous 800 percent in 2007 before turning around and losing 50 percent in 2008, were almost evenly split in terms of ownership between those managers that run GARP funds and those that run core value funds—both had about $2 billion in shares apiece. They're followed by the growth and core growth groups, who, combined, have about $2.6 billion in shares as of the middle of 2009.

Another speculative favorite is Dendreon, a popular biotechnology holding among day-traders between 2006 and 2009 who were waiting for the company's prostate cancer treatment to be approved. This company's shares also were held in substantive amounts by growth and value investors. Fidelity Investments, as of September 30, 2009, had the stock in more than 40 funds, mostly in its growth-oriented small-cap funds, but also included it in eight funds that are described as "core value" funds, so the stock has a presence in both conservative and more aggressive investments.

This isn't to suggest there's one right answer with each investment. Any stock that is considered a prime growth candidate but has hit a rough patch, losing a substantial amount of its value, is fodder for the value investor. But it doesn't do an individual much good if his 401(k) plan owns a growth manager and a value manager that have a substantial overlap in their holdings. The better strategy would be to merely buy an index fund, and diversify the rest through funds concentrated on investments that are meant to be less correlated, such as hard assets (or shares of companies that own hard assets), along with international stocks, bonds, and short-term instruments such as CDs or money-market funds. Here's a quick tip: Go look at the funds you're holding in your individual retirement account or 401(k) or 403(b) plan, and see how many you have. If you've got ten or more you're probably engaging in quite a bit of duplication to begin with. After that, you should go to the Securities and Exchange Commission's Web site and look up the funds in question. They all file quarterly reports that include a list of their holdings, and you can scroll through and see if any common names come up in more than a few funds. More than likely, there is overlap. Following that you'll have to get about the task of selling off holdings that are trading too similarly to others. If you have index funds, you can probably sell the large-cap funds; if you own total market index funds, the small-cap funds you have are less important. The growth and value distinctions are nice, but they may be too granular as well. With that excess capital you'll be able to deploy it elsewhere—buying asset classes that are substantially different than others, such as inflation-protected Treasury bonds, bond funds that invest in emerging markets, and hard assets like gold or oil. This will move you away from an excessively equity-oriented portfolio. Of course, this isn't a panacea when markets all start to act similarly.

Moving Together

To quote Ralph Fiennes in the film *In Bruges*, this just gets worse. What's happened in recent years is that assets generally thought to be independent of one another have started to move in lockstep.

It's one thing for Standard & Poor's various stock industries to exhibit similar trading patterns. It is another entirely for asset classes considered completely different to march together, and that's what has happened over the last years of this decade. It's a phenomena that has only intensified as the credit crisis erupted, and the breadth and depth of the world's structural imbalances (that is, too much debt, overconsumption in certain countries, and not enough investment in business) determines that it could continue.

Bianco took a group of 12 completely different assets, including Brazilian stocks, Chinese stocks, an index of volatility in the fixed-income market, the euro, the yields on bonds issued in emerging market countries, crude oil, and prominent commodities and freight rates indexes, and found that as of January 2009, the least correlated index to the S&P 500—the MOVE Index, which measures volatility in bonds—was correlated 64 percent of the time. Removing that from the group, and the least correlated was the Chinese stock market, which had a correlation of 76 percent.

Now, these markets do tend to shift, and in more normalized times, they will once again move independently of each other—some of them were near polar opposites of the S&P 500 in the 1990s and early 2000s. But their positive correlation now makes it difficult for investors to achieve diversification, because money tends to do one of two things: flow into all of these assets, or flow away from all of them.

This is a function of investor risk appetite. Either the mass majority of investors are fleeing in the direction of risky assets, or they're running away from them (those not correlated include short-term cash instruments like money market funds, as well as Treasury bills, but those instruments do not protect against inflation, so they have their own drawbacks). Bianco traces this back to Fed policy again. "Fed policy has been driving the financial markets more than anything else," he said. "It's one big macro theme: We put rates too low, and the markets boom, and we raise them and they bust."

This does not, however, mean that every asset is correlated. Certain assets continue to exhibit little or no relationship with the purchases that make up the bulk of one's portfolio, that being large-cap stocks. These assets themselves do not generally sport the kind of returns that the equity market does, making them poorer choices to take a larger portion of one's investments. Those include short-term debt as well as bonds—government debt currently has a negative correlation with the stock market, moving in the opposite direction of equities.

Foreign stocks have shown an increasing correlation with large-cap U.S. names, but the ongoing erosion in the dollar increases their value and protects investors from deterioration in the U.S. currency. The same can be said for stocks of hard assets, such as gold or oil. Metals and other commodities are driven largely by supply and demand considerations separate from the bulk of the economy and therefore are not as well correlated either.

The challenge for the individual is this, then: successfully putting together a portfolio that achieves a level of diversification that can help one offset losses in one asset with gains in another one. It's not enough to have different assets—they must be consistent in that they diverge from the rest of the market. As Bianco has pointed out, that's been a tall order for most investors in the last few years, thanks to the tight relationship between the euro, stocks, commodities, emerging markets, and even certain debt instruments. A 2004 Rydex Investments publication noted that certain assets were strong choices for low correlation with stocks: equity inverse products, those that seek to do the opposite of the stock market, as well as fixed income inverse products, and managed futures. Leveraged fixed income and real estate investment trusts also had a relatively loose relationship with stocks, although it was stronger than equity inverse exchange-traded funds and other such products.[14]

Overall, though, for most investors, the idea of diversification was to own a relatively predictable mix between stocks and bonds, mostly weighted in favor of stocks, a few bonds thrown in, and maybe some international stocks for good measure. That's not enough diversification, and left alone, eventually stocks would have likely come to dominate the portfolio, leaving investors more exposed to eventual downturns when the market invariably corrected (which it did, violently, in 2008 and 2009). Rob Arnott of Research Affiliates wrote in January 2010 that further diversification—between 16 equal-weighted asset classes would have produced a return of about 6.8 percent annualized in the 2000s decade (the "Aughts") because it would have had additional exposure to emerging markets classes, to commodities, to short-term debt, to inflation-protected securities, and other investments. Meanwhile, a simple division between stocks and bonds (60 percent to 40 percent) would have returned 2.3 percent annualized, in large part because of a lousy performance from large-cap equity throughout the decade.[15]

With Treasury and corporate debt having rallied dramatically in the last few years, it's possible that those investments will drag in the next decade. A ten-year period where bonds are lackluster and stocks do well is likely going to be more fruitful for investors than the last ten, when stocks were the drag and bonds did well, but that's not an assumption anyone should bank on. Because the traditional stock/bond division isn't going to be enough, and with the increasing availability of investing strategies through individual retirement accounts and 401(k) plans, there's greater opportunity for true diversification of assets. This process is much easier now thanks to the proliferation of exchange-traded funds, which we'll discuss at more length in a coming chapter, but essentially, they're stocklike investments bought and sold on public exchanges that allow an investor to gain exposure to a bit more esoteric asset classes, such as stock funds that seek to do the opposite of what the market is doing, or corporate debt funds (which can still be purchased as mutual funds—some of these may be a better option than ETFs), or commodity-oriented funds.

But since it's not enough to simply divide everything up into a bunch of categories, that's where a bit of active management comes into play. This isn't day-trading, and doesn't involve obsessively looking at the screens every day even if you're not trading, either. It involves paying attention and putting together a system that will allow you to keep your portfolio balanced, instead of overly weighted in already expensive assets, which is what most of us got used to seeing in the 2000s.

There are plenty of people who believe you should sit back and let your investments ride until the day you retire, but that's not going to work, not if you end up hitting a massive bear market just before it's time for you to shift assets to more conservative investments. Nor is wildly trading things back and forth and destroying your returns through excessive transaction fees. At its simplest, selling the parts of your portfolio that have done better than expected to maintain the optimum allocation will put you ahead of most other people in terms of attention to your portfolio. Such a move protects you—sure, you'll be losing ground at times when the markets are going straight up, but you'll also be consistently reducing your exposure to assets that have outdone others, and that has value when markets take a turn for the worse.

As always, however, there are those looking for the better mousetrap. There are a number of people out there trying to figure out what the optimal amount of activity is for you and me—believing it's something more than doing nothing, a bit less than constant action. Utilizing such advice involves becoming comfortable with the idea of making occasional sales in one's investments that don't have to do with taxes, college payments, or retirement, however. They're the kind of moves that everyone cautions against in lieu of "not fighting the market" or whatever piece of advice that people cling to lest they have to make a decision—and they're also fraught with peril. Is there enough of a benefit in transactions made other than rebalancing sales for you to actually make strategic decisions about your portfolio? Some believe so—let's explore it a bit more.

Boiling It Down

- Diversification is essential. You need to look beyond simply diversifying between different types of stock investments, however, as many stock mutual funds, whether grouped by size, style of investing, or sector, often mimic one another.

- The best move you can make is to try to avoid overlap, or "fake diversification." A total market index fund will cover most of the market—there's no need to double up with another small-cap index fund or another large-cap index fund when your money is better spent in other places.

- Do you own a lot of stock funds? Go to the SEC's Web site and find their list of holdings. If they hold a number of similar stocks, you're not getting enough diversification. Sell the higher-cost one and keep the lower-cost one.

Endnotes

[1]Author interview.

[2]Bianco Research LLC, "It's All the Same Trade," commentary, January 27, 2009.

[3]Author interview.

[4]Author interview.

[5]Author interview.

[6]NYSE Web site, http://testwww.nyse.com/about/listed/funds.html.

[7]Standard & Poor's data.

[8]NYSE statistical data.

[9]Jeffrey Stangl, Ben Jacobsen, and Nuttawat Visaltanachoti, "Sector Rotation over Business Cycles," Massey University, August 2009.

[10]CXO Advisory Group blog, "Do Any Sector ETFs Reliably Lead or Lag the Market?" http://www.cxoadvisory.com/blog/internal/blog12-24-09/.

[11]"Sector Rotation and Monetary Conditions," Mitchell Conover, associate professor of finance at the University of Richmond, along with Robert Johnson of the CFA Institute, Jeffrey Mercer of Texas Tech University, and Gerald Jensen of Northern Illinois, June 25, 2007.

[12]Standard & Poor's data.

[13]Thomson Reuters data.

[14]"Investing: More of a Challenge," Rydex Investments, 2004.

[15]"Was It Really a Lost Decade," Research Affiliates newsletter, January 2010.

7

Buying a Portfolio—And Selling It

"Regardless of the frequency of rebalancing, fidelity to asset-allocation targets proves important as a means of risk control and return enhancement."
David Swensen, head of Yale University's endowment

The data previously cited about the long-term prowess of stocks does suggest that someone with an investment horizon of about 70 years (so if you're about 13 years old and just got a bunch of bonds for your Bar Mitzvah, I'm talking to you) would do well to stick with indexing and leave it at that. But it's not a realistic option for those looking at the last ten years of investment returns and seeing the paltry gains in all funds to say that leaving one's money alone is enough to satisfy anyone. It's simply human nature that a lost decade like this one makes an investor antsy, particularly with the limited number of offerings of indexes that are less sensitive to the impact of market capitalization. The 1990s were a time when anyone was a genius: Stock pickers did well, but passive investors who were content with indexes sure could look at several years of 20-percent-plus growth and not feel too upset about it.

But that hasn't been the case for some time. "The fact is that investors are human beings and when you tell them they have less money than they had ten years ago they're likely not to go for it," said John Bollinger, president of Bollinger Capital and inventor of Bollinger Bands, a strategy that gauges market sentiment as to when to buy and sell shares. "When you inflation-adjust those numbers, they look terrible."[1]

Bollinger and others suggest that some level of active management can be applied somehow to try to beat the market. Studies do prove this, even from the mutual fund company most well-known for indexing strategies—Vanguard of Valley Forge, Pennsylvania. In fact, about 60 percent of Vanguard's funds are actively managed. In a 2009 study, they found that in periods of relative calm—such as the 1990s—index funds have it all over those in the market trying to time the good and bad, with 69 percent of managers underperforming the Dow Jones Wilshire 5000 Index.[2]

But that flipped on its head in the 2000s. For the ten-year period ended in 2008, just 34 percent of managers underperformed indexes, while the rest managed to outperform. Part of this is because large-cap growth stocks, such as the Microsofts of the world, trailed badly in the last decade, and they make up the bulk of the market capitalization of the popular indexes such as the S&P 500 and the Wilshire 5000. (Again, another reason to try to find noncapitalization weighted indexes.) As a result, it was a time when active managers selecting small-cap value stocks could make greater headway. So where's the problem? Once again, the issue is one of cost. If the average actively managed fund is costing an investor around 3 percentage points, that's going to eat up returns, and suddenly an outperforming manager is struggling to keep up. "Most actively managed strategies fail because they charge too much," said Fran Kinniry, head of Vanguard's investment strategy group. "You probably find 60 to 65 percent can win, but when you look at after-fee they do not win."[3]

Vanguard manages to combat this by keeping costs low, even in its actively managed funds, charging about two-tenths to one-half of a percentage point more than the company's index funds. The average fund charges more than 1 percent in up-front fees, before trading costs are even accounted for. It may be that indexes aren't the be-all end-all, but their cost structure usually sets them apart. What's interesting is that Kinniry still notes that indexing is likely to come out ahead in the end over an actively managed portfolio unless the investor in question has the fortitude to get into the market at its most difficult moments, such as in February or March 2009. He notes that after hitting a 12-year-low on March 9, 2009, major averages gained 40 percent within the first 40 trading days of hitting that low, at a time when most investors were likely to be running away from the market. Domestic equity flows were negative in five of the six months prior to March 2009, according to the Investment Company Institute, which tracks mutual fund statistics. And March 2009 saw net outflows of $17.29 billion from U.S. equity funds, according to the ICI. Flows into equity funds only started to pick up a bit more in the late first quarter of 2010, almost a year after the rally had begun and those in the market had watched major averages rise by 70 percent.

It suggests again that the retail investor tends to be poor at timing the market, as this was the most opportune time for an investor to be buying, once again, at the time of greatest pain. Those in index funds could be assured that they were at least in the market.

So the performance of actively managed funds means that in an environment of uncertainty likely to persist for another several years, it's best to go in that direction, right? The trouble lies in two places: the disclosed fees, which are easy to figure out, and the other fees—trading costs. As time has worn on in the stock market, turnover has increased dramatically; the average mutual fund now turns over most of its portfolio within a year rather than holding for several years, and this is a major bite into costs—returns have to justify the additional activity.

It's relatively easy to document this sort of thing when it comes to retail investors. As mentioned earlier, Terrence Odean and Brad Barber found how the average household was outperforming the market between 1991 and 1996, but fell short once trading costs and commissions were added in.

This sort of thing hadn't been effectively studied in mutual funds until very recently, but a trio of professors—Roger Edelen of Echo Investment Advisors, Richard Evans of Boston College, and Gregory Kadlec of Virginia Tech—managed the trick in the last couple of years as well, publishing a study in 2007 that showed how trading costs are eating up returns for professionals also.

While their estimates of trading costs can be disputed, they also found that most mutual funds are killing themselves with those costs, which were even worse than up-front fees. In some instances, the expense ratio still outweighed the trading cost: Funds investing primarily in large-cap stocks sported a mean expense ratio of 1.12 percent, while the estimated annual trading costs were 0.77 percent.[4]

But when looking at funds concentrated on small-cap investments, things get a lot worse: Expense ratios were about 1.34 percent, but the estimated trading costs were a ridiculous 2.85 percent. So that's more than four percentage points of outperformance needed just to surpass the market average, and as Vanguard's data shows, there aren't a lot of managers that can achieve this.

The managers who do the worst, interestingly enough, are the largest funds. What's so distressing about this is that they're the ones more likely to attract the bulk of investors, either through 401(k) plans or because of reputation. Trading costs increase as the fund grows, according to Evans of Boston College. "If you have a million dollars under management and you're trading 100 percent of your portfolio, well, a million bucks seems like a lot to me but in terms of moving the price, the impact in trading is not very large," said Evans. "Once I get to a billion dollars my trades are going to move the market, so as I start to get out of a position you're driving the price down and when you get in, you're driving the price way up."[5]

As each successive trade pushes a stock higher or lower, it increases those costs for that particular fund. It's akin to turning an aircraft carrier—it's going to make some waves. The largest funds trade less than smaller ones—with trading volume of about 147 percent of their fund in a year, compared with about 188 percent for smaller funds—but the cost per trade is much larger, and so the cost comes out the same—about 1.44 percentage points of annual trading costs per year. All of this work just to fall short of major averages.

Rebalancing—Your Best Friend

By now we have established that mutual fund managers are more often than not going to fail to outperform the broader index, usually because costs will eat up their profits. So it leaves an investor in the position of Newman in the "Seinfeld" episode, trying to find the magic formula that would allow him to ship thousands of recyclable bottles to Michigan (where bottle deposits are 10 cents, rather than 5 cents in most other states) without incurring the heavy gasoline costs that would destroy his returns. It's about as easily solved, too, and you're not saddled with the advice of the hapless Cosmo Kramer.

Trading more frequently doesn't seem to be the answer, either. So beginning with an index fund as one's stock allocation makes the most sense due to the favorable cost factors. The rest of one's portfolio will be allocated to bonds, cash, commodities, real estate, bank loans, or a few other assets discussed later. The question then becomes, what is the proper level of active management for investors interested in trying to maximize returns?

This section takes you through the most passive—simple rebalancing, done automatically once a year—through more active levels of management that include chart-based market timing and those who are attempting to mimic the portfolios of people who actually do seem to have a knack for being good stock pickers (and there really aren't too many of these). What we'll see is that there are many folks who aren't giving up—who believe there's a way to consistently come out ahead of the market over a long period of time, a place where many have tried and failed. For my part, I tend to stick to the idea that simple rebalancing and occasional selling of certain highly valued assets is the best, most prudent approach, without getting particularly fancy, and then of course shifting your allocation when you've got the kind of time horizon that demands you get more conservative.

The argument for rebalancing a portfolio is simple: If an investor believes their level of risk appetite and their goals match up best with, say, dividing investments into 60 percent stock and 40 percent bonds, after a while, given varying returns for these investments, stocks or bonds are going to start to dominate the fund more. A $100,000 investment split in this way that posts a 20 percent return for stocks and five percent for bonds is going to rise to $72,000 in stocks and $42,000 in bonds. That investment has grown to $114,000, and the stock portion is now 63 percent of the portfolio, and that's more than an investor wants. A bit of selling once a year will bring that back in line, and should the more expensive asset—likely to be the stock market—experience a pullback, it will not be felt as much in one's holdings because of the previous rebalancing effort. (See box for explanation.)

Let's do the simple math to see how rebalancing can help you in the event of a severe downturn. For simple mathematical purposes, let's say you've got $100,000 as we mentioned, split 60-40 in favor of stocks. And we'll assume stocks post five consecutive years of 15 percent gains, and bonds gain 5 percent—until year six, when stocks lose 25 percent, and bonds gain 7 percent. A portfolio that never rebalances will see the assets increase as such:

	STOCKS	BONDS
Year 1	69,000	42,000
Year 2	79,350	44,100
Year 3	91,252.50	46,305
Year 4	104,940.38	48,620.25
Year 5	120,681.43	51,051.26
Year 6 (-25%)	90,511.07	53,603.83

This portfolio ends with 144,114.90 after six years. Now let's look at someone who rebalances—and every year shifts assets so they have 60 percent allocated to stocks.

	STOCKS	BONDS
Year 1	66,600	44,400
Year 2	73,926	49,284
Year 3	82,057.96	54,705.24
Year 4	91,084.22	60,722.82
Year 5	104,746.90	63,758.96
Year 6	78,560.14	68,222.08

This portfolio ends with a balance of 146,782.20 after six years. And this example, by itself, may be flawed because it assumes five stellar years of returns for stocks without interruption and decent gains for bonds every year until bonds do a bit better in the wake of a stock-market sell-off. A period of heightened stock returns without the consequences of a bear market (and bear markets tend to happen) will produce more inferior results.

David Swensen, the investment strategist who oversees investing for Yale University's endowment, is a big proponent of rebalancing. An article he wrote noted that in fiscal 2003, Yale "executed approximately $3.8 billion in rebalancing trades, roughly evenly split between purchases and sales. Net profit from rebalancing amounted to approximately $26 million, representing a 1.6 percent incremental return on the $1.6 billion domestic equity portfolio."[6]

There are still concerns with this approach, particularly when rebalancing is used frequently, as it can come back to hit individual investors. In a market that continues to trend upward consistently, or downward consistently, rebalancing trades can reduce risk, but they can hurt returns, because investors will be consistently reducing their holdings in the investment that is doing well, and because there's a cost to these trades (further behooving you to find the lowest-cost option possible, or taking advantage of a discount brokerage's offer of dozens of free trades by parceling them out as infrequently as possible). Still, during the bull run of the 1990s, an investor would be shedding the very asset that was outperforming in favor of the more sluggish returns of bonds; during bear markets, investors would be doubling down on stocks amid ugly slumps. "The U.S. stock market's steady upward surge during the mid- to late-1990s was an example of a trending market. Rebalancing produced lower returns than a portfolio that was never rebalanced," wrote analysts at Vanguard in a recent study.[7]

The 1990s market may, however, have been an aberration. Stocks moved consistently higher for most of that decade, exploding into the end of a multiyear run with several years of 20-plus percent in returns. The 1960s and 1970s were nowhere near as kind, and of course, this most recent decade hasn't been friendly to those who let it ride, either.

Overall, it seems there's a middle ground for rebalancing. Quarterly rebalancing of a portfolio, assuming a five percent deviation from your targeted allocation (say, 60 percent equities, 40 percent bonds), gives you a disciplined schedule to work from, but doesn't incur unnecessary trading if your assets haven't returned enough to warrant the rebalancing. From 1960 to 2003, quarterly rebalancing produced a return of 9.669 percent annually, slightly better than monthly or annual rebalancing, according to Vanguard. Such portfolios were also a bit less volatile than those rebalanced just one time a year, and produced better returns than the monthly rebalancing schedule.

If anything, the data supports limited efforts to shift one's portfolio so it reflects the intended allocation, but preferably with a high bar so excessive trading costs are not incurred. Swensen maintains that this is meant to be a way to impose discipline. For many of you, this kind of approach can serve as a perfect structure for reevaluating your investments or making simple changes—you know you're going to look at it quarterly, but no more than that and you're going to have to see significant movement to justify changing things. But it also means you're giving yourself a chance to see how things are going instead of forgetting about it and only taking a gander at your portfolio when things are going haywire, and everything's been lost. Make no mistake—simple rebalancing will not prevent or avoid bear markets. But a portfolio that's constantly shifting assets away from those that have outperformed is more protected than that of one that has never done such a thing.

Timing the Market

The once-a-year "set it and forget it" style of rebalancing has its merits because it does not require the investor in question to make judgments about the market. It assumes a certain risk tolerance and sticks with that regardless of the environment. Some managers advocate a more opportunistic approach to rebalancing, the kind of thing Swensen of the Yale endowment seems to actively do.

This strategy has a bad name, though—market timing. And the reason it has such a horrific reputation is again more a result of practice than it is theory: It's because so many investors are just awful at executing it. Just as investors are more likely to buy mutual funds when they reach their peak in terms of investing prowess (and thus dooming themselves to inevitable subpar returns later on), they also have very poor judgment when it comes to effectively buying and selling the market.

Naturally many professionals advocate such an approach, seeing it as the key to outperformance in their portfolios. In see-saw times, it's hard to justify sitting back passively, as Vitaliy Katsenelson, president of Investment Management Associates Inc. in Denver, Colorado, puts it: "You have to be proactive in buying and selling." He, of course, actively manages portfolios for his clients, and detractors of the argument suggest that most fund managers are unable to add excess return because of costs and the inability to maintain an edge over a long period of time.[8]

From a theoretical level, it makes sense that there are some sectors and some asset classes that outperform markets at different times in the business cycle. Researchers from Massey University took a look at the idea of buying certain sectors at certain times, but found the simpler strategy of continuously buying stocks—moving out of stocks only during the early portion of the recession—is superior to most other strategies that involve buying stocks more sensitive to the economy (semiconductors, construction, and equipment companies) when demand is rising, and moving to things that are always needed when demand is falling (utilities, health care, toothpaste). They found that such a strategy—where investors buy stocks through the early, middle, and late parts of an expansion, shift to cash for the early recession, and then back into stocks late in a recession, would outdo the market by an average 7 percent.

Mike Trovato, product manager at Pacific Investment Management Co. Inc., argued for a similar approach in a November 2009 commentary. He noted that essentially, investors should feel free to invest in riskier assets during the expansion and late part of a recession, shifting to Treasury securities during the early part of a recession. In the early and middle part of the expansions that took place between 1988 and 2008, emerging market debt was the best investing vehicle for returns, outdoing high-yield debt, equities, convertible bonds, and Treasury securities. Late-expansion, stocks were the best performers.[9] But at the onset of the recession, it was time to get into the government bond market and leave everything else behind. On average, Treasuries produced an average return during those periods of 10.62 percent, while all other asset classes lost money during that period. Treasuries continued to do well through the late part of the recession, but now they were once again bested by high yield debt and other kinds of debt as investors turned to the idea of greater risk.

What's the problem with all of this as a strategy? It's predicated on your understanding that a recession has arrived, and in December 2007, when the recession started, very few of us got that idea, particularly as markets had peaked just two months earlier. In fact, most were convinced the market's problems were minor, confined to subprime mortgage loans and bad debts in various economies that had overborrowed when their currencies were highly valued. Of course, this proved to be a disastrous assumption, and every asset class was roundly kicked in the rear, with the exception of (you guessed it) the Treasury market, which rallied as bonds hit record lows.

But more and more professional investors are heeding the lessons learned in 2008 and 2009, and believing somehow, they have to take a different approach. They're instead taking the notion of shifting assets from high-performing classes to lower-performing ones to a more granular level. This emerging approach to portfolio management is known as "tactical asset allocation," and maybe that's a fancy way of saying "market timing," but top professionals argue that reallocation based on set parameters, be it relative strength of a particular stock sector, or certain technical patterns, can save investors headaches. "A total of 99.9 percent of the industry is very negative on market timing and stock picking, and research shows that both people and professionals are consistently horrendous at it," said Mebane Faber, co-founder and portfolio manager at Cambria Investment Management in Los Angeles.[10]

But Faber notes that in the 20th century, all of the G-7 economies—the largest world economies including the U.S., U.K., Japan, and Germany—saw their stock markets experience a period where they lost 75 percent of their value. And in such a case, an investor then needs a 300 percent gain just to get back to even! That's a 10 percent return over the next 15 years—and many people don't have a 15-year horizon, such as retirees who were expecting a nest egg until they ran into the 2007-2008 debacle in the markets. And plenty of markets don't give you 10 percent a year for 15 years—

invariably there will be a correction in that time that makes breaking even from horrific losses more difficult. It behooves people to try to avoid such fallow periods, and it makes it easier to do so when you're not invested in individual stocks that can completely disappear, but instead in a number of asset classes with an eye to flexibility.

He advocates a relatively simple approach to market timing. It involves looking at one's assets at the end of every month and determining whether stocks have risen above the ten-month moving average or fallen below it. Moving averages are calculated by taking the closing prices in a particular average over a period of time, and adjusting that every day or week or month to take into account each new piece of information as time passes. They're used frequently as a way to gauge trends in certain markets. When an index falls below a certain moving average it is taken as a bad sign. So, if the S&P 500 is trading higher than its ten-month moving average (the average closing price over the past ten months), stay invested in stocks. When it falls below this level, it's time to sell and go into cash or some similar equivalent. And then, once the market has again moved above the 200-day moving average, it's time to buy.

This does appear to produce better returns: Between 1900 and 2008, the S&P 500 posted an average annual return of 9.21 percent, with nearly 18 percent volatility (the percentage an index may be expected to move up or down in one year). But a timing approach boosts that return to 10.45 percent, and reduces volatility to about 12 percent. Such an approach would have gotten investors out of the market within the long bear market of the 1930s, and the decline would have been reduced to about 42 percent from nearly 84 percent.

Bull markets, similarly, would have not been as fruitful for the market timing investor—investors would have gotten out before the market peak. Faber's data shows that investors in the 1940s and 1950s would have trailed the market averages due to the strategy's penchant for pulling out of stocks at what appears to be a time of overvaluation—but one in which stocks continue to gain strength. The 1990s are similar: This roaring period would have been somewhat missed in Faber's approach—gaining about 13 percent on an annual basis, compared with more than 18 percent for those who simply held the market.

On the upside, investors would have stayed out of shares after the inevitable decline—the 2008 fall of 37 percent in the S&P 500 would have not fazed someone subscribing to Faber's system, as that investor would have posted a 1.3 percent positive gain for the year, having jumped out of stocks on the last day of 2007 in favor of Treasury bills.

So when does this approach really shine? In see-saw periods, such as the 1970s and 2000s—periods that included terrible bear markets and rousing bull markets, sometimes all within a year. The average annual return during the Disco Era was 5.88 percent, but timing the market boosts that to 8.4 percent. And the index lost 3.6 percent, on average, between 2000 and 2008, while the more nimble investor looking at the moving average gained 6.3 percent.

The method, at least according to Faber's data, works for other asset classes as well—investors would have boosted returns in foreign stocks to about 11 percent from 9 percent between 1973 and 2008, and the same goes for someone in global commodities indexes, where returns improved to 11.2 percent from 8.7 percent, again reducing volatility, and real estate investment trusts, which improved to 11.7 percent from 8.5 percent. (The difference for long-term Treasury debt is miniscule, by contrast.)

This system isn't fool-proof, obviously. Commissions, fees, and taxes come into play, particularly as investors are looking at making three or four trades a year from one asset to Treasury bills and back again, according to Faber, in a paper he wrote for the *Journal of Wealth Management.*[11] Obviously, using index funds and ETFs will keep costs low, and commissions should remain low with a limited number of trades, particularly in an era where ETFs are tradable without a commission. Taxes are likely to impose a bigger bite on investors, which makes implementing such a strategy in taxable accounts potentially cost-prohibitive. A tax-free account such as a 401(k) is a more ideal place for such a strategy.

Right now, the chief problem folks like Faber face is convincing clients that tactical asset allocation, or as it is more problematically known, market timing, makes any kind of sense at all. Investors have been schooled in buying and holding investments, frightened—for good reason—that they'll make decisions to alter the mix of their investments at all the wrong times. Furthermore, this system has only been back-tested, and it remains to be seen whether such a strategy will withstand periods where the market teeter-totters for a long time, giving off false signals on getting in or out of the market, or if it goes into another extended run similar to the 1982-2000 period that demands investors remain invested at all times.

However, the principle behind it—that investors shouldn't blindly assume that the markets will cure all ills over a long period of time—is a sound premise, and it's not been one that you and I have been able to accept more readily in recent years. After all, for so long, stocks continued to go up and up, and we allowed ourselves to assign blame for the brief recession in 2000-2001 to overvalued technology companies and horrific terrorist attacks, thus rationalizing its existence away. Getting back on the "all stock" horse was easy. That's harder to say now, with the Dow in 2010 still struggling to stay above the 10,000 mark, a level it first surpassed more than 12 years previous.

Now, however, you can sense a sea change. Many investors are piling their assets into bonds, regardless of the market's fantastic rally that started in March 2009. That's because the idea of another ten years of volatile markets that essentially go nowhere isn't going to make anyone happy. "It's self-preservation," one UBS Securities advisor told *Registered Rep.* magazine in August 2009. "I have to make my clients money no matter what kind of market we're in or I'm out of business."[12] (Disclosure: I worked at this magazine between 2001 and 2005.)

Implementing an effective strategy that shifts money from one asset to another based on market levels isn't easy, however. "The key is to have the courage to sell what everyone loves and thinks will perform brilliantly and buy what everyone fears and thinks is headed for oblivion," said Rob Arnott, who uses tactical asset allocation in his portfolios, among other management approaches. Without that, he says, "you're better off with simple rebalancing."

The approach has its detractors. Burton Malkiel, author of *A Random Walk Down Wall Street*, said in the *Registered Rep.* article that professionals are no better, as "most managers tend to be most bullish at the top, bearish at the bottom." A trio of professors published a paper confirming this in 2007: They noted that whatever the benefits of having a financial advisor were, superior skills at timing the market was not one of them, and in fact, their picks tended to underperform the market, even before fees were included in the mix. "We find no evidence that, in aggregate, brokers provide superior asset allocation advice that helps their investors time the market," wrote Professors Daniel Bergstresser, John Chalmers, and Peter Tufano. "While we cannot observe the asset allocation skills of individual brokers nor the degree to which brokers fashion customized portfolios for their clients, the aggregate asset allocations show no advantages among the broker-sold funds."[13] Perhaps not wanting to be too harsh, the trio conceded that other benefits—helping people apply a savings discipline, realizing tax benefits for clients—might offset some of the costs of the assets purchased (and the up-front fee demanded by advisors), but the hard evidence that relates to costs shows that advisors aren't any better at this, and they add in a middle man that charges more money.

Fran Kinniry of Vanguard, meanwhile, said the firm manages funds in a tactical manner as well, although judging by the public speeches from Vanguard's storied founder John Bogle, one wouldn't know they had anything subject to active management. In reality, more than half of the firm's assets are being managed as such, and

Kinniry still says their belief is that "most actively managed strategies fail because they charge too much." Vanguard's actively managed funds have a lower expense ratio, which makes outperformance more likely, but certainly not a slam-dunk.

Nevertheless, Kinniry and others recognize that the Holy Grail—outperformance—beckons many an investor. Few have positive expectations for the investing environment in coming years, something we'll discuss in a forthcoming chapter, and because of that, a raging bull market similar to the 1990 to 1999 period, or the prolonged steadiness of the 1980s/1990s seems unlikely, even though investors have already experienced this for the last decade. And with that expectation comes the desire to avoid getting caught in a trap where passive investments lead investors down the wrong path if there's a way—some kind of way—to avoid that.

The Buffett Way

The search for the better mousetrap has motivated many, including Mazin Jadallah, chief executive officer of investment research service AlphaClone, which he co-founded with Cambria's Mebane Faber. Jadallah describes himself as a "very frustrated retail investor," particularly in light of his impressive background: an MBA from Rollins College, stints at Open TV and Time Warner in analysis and corporate development. But managing his portfolio just wasn't working out.

"I have a high opinion of myself," he said. "I've got an MBA in finance, I worked at Time Warner for (former CEO) Dick Parsons, and I've done strategy and M&A and corporate development work. I know what the value of our company is, but I couldn't pick a stock to save my life. Is it asymmetry? Is it that I don't have time or the money to do the kind of tight analysis to pick winners? I think for a whole host of reasons, most people are not very good at picking stocks."[14]

However, he and Faber weren't convinced there was nobody out there who didn't outperform markets consistently. If anything, there was Warren Buffett, and while the famed CEO of Berkshire Hathaway Inc. is not constrained by the parameters of a mutual fund, Jadallah felt there had to be some way to track Mr. Buffett, and that there had to be others who had demonstrated consistent prowess in picking equities that would do better than the rest of the market. Among those he named were Greenlight Capital's David Einhorn, Chris Davis of Davis Advisors, Daniel Loeb of Third Point LLC, and the various people who were schooled under Tiger Management's Julian Robertson.

Of course, access to these hedge fund managers is limited to those with connections and a lot of money, but AlphaClone is trying another method—searching through 13-F filings, regular submissions on holdings by hedge fund managers to the Securities and Exchange Commission—and combing through them for data on holdings of these big investors. The investment research firm then constructs portfolios based on the most current information about these holdings. Using their best information they've found that these portfolios, when back-tested, can outperform dramatically when compared with the market. And instead of following just one manager, like Buffett, a subscriber can follow several managers at once to reduce the risk of one firm's blow-up (after all, a number of prominent hedge funds melted down during the 2008-2009 disaster, and nobody would have been all that thrilled with mimicking the destructive portfolio that Long-Term Capital Management saw whittled away to nothing in 1997).

Jadallah says the company doesn't track underperformers—it would be pointless to create clones that match lousy managers. And some hedge funds have proven more problematic than others to create clones out of because of massive levels of trading in these funds, heavy usage of derivatives, certain types of short sales, arbitrage strategies, and other tricks sophisticated managers use to hide their positions. Some hedge funds, such as Renaissance Capital or SAC Capital, have generally poor performing clones because of this. "That doesn't mean (SAC) doesn't do well," Jadallah says. "But our whole point is from a retail investor's perspective: Any investor who is not in the SAC fund doesn't pay attention to their 13-F disclosures or stock moves—the back-tests show the clone wouldn't do well."

There are other concerns as well: AlphaClone, which went live in December 2008, doesn't have access to the manager itself, and a 45-day waiting period to file with regulators after the end of a quarter is the equivalent of delivering e-mail by Pony Express—careers have been lost on stocks held for an extra week, never mind a month-and-a-half. By then, the hedge fund manager could have sold that position and every other holding in their fund and gone in an entirely different direction.

It's easy to see how AlphaClone could gain popularity with the legion of investors looking for a shorthand way to invest the way pros do (the basic cost of membership is a mere $30 a month, with plans to charge as much as $100 a month, according to Jadallah). It's because we're willing to move the earth to find that Holy Grail, that person who will outperform all others for long periods of time, and not just what seem like extended lucky runs of six to eight years,

It's a task that a man named Ken Kam has been trying to accomplish for most of the last decade. Kam is the founder of Marketocracy, a Web-based product that has tracked portfolios for most of the decade, not from the Buffett types, but regular people who manage their own money and who contribute their picks to Marketocracy's data. Currently, there are more than 80,000 people managing more than 100,000 model portfolios from more than 130 countries around the world on the Web site.

Kam's firm has found that certain people are better at picking stocks and making money than others. Unlike those who believe that ultimately, trying to beat the market is a loser's game, where eventually everyone falls to the middle, Kam is of the belief that money can be made consistently. And individuals who think they have the chops can sign up on their site (for free) to run model portfolios. (Premium membership adds access to advanced portfolio management tools and reports on what others are doing.)

These are model portfolios—signing up gives an investor a fictional $1 million to invest, and each member can register up to ten funds. The company publishes rankings of its best performers on its site—as of March 31, 2010, the leader over the last five years was a man named Mike Koza, an engineer by trade who over five years has an annualized return of 38.6 percent.[15] A few others are listed on the site, with their biographies, and then others with top performing funds include the likes of people who go by "bravedave" or "the_barnacle," which are not the names of fund managers one is going to find in a mutual fund prospectus any time soon. Nonetheless, they do suggest that those with a sufficient amount of time can do well, although once again, these portfolios are models, and the company's disclaimer notes that "since the trades have not actually been executed, the results may under- or over-compensate for the impact, if any, of certain market factors, such as the effect of limited trading liquidity."

Kam recognizes that there are no certainties in the business. Bill Miller is the toast of Wall Street for more than a decade, and then people don't consider him fit to wipe their shoes. Those in the market are, of course, only as good as their next call. But Kam is still not convinced that the "mechanistic" approach, one that advocates indexing, rebalancing, and not much more, is the way to go.

"People have tried to take all of the judgment out of it, and I don't think it's possible to take all of the judgment out of it," he said. "In the end, it comes down to either you need to develop judgment and know what kinds of judgments you're good at, or find people who have track records that are better than yours and those are the people you should delegate to." He notes that the market's 40 percent drop in 2008-2009 was not something many could foresee, and even fewer were counting on, and unless the investor in question is within shouting distance of their senior prom, the long-term average is of little comfort. "People can't afford to have the next ten years be like the last ten," he said.[16]

The most disconcerting aspect of that statement? The next ten years may, indeed, be similar to the past ten, particularly if you're primarily invested in the U.S. It's why Kam stays in business. It's why people are going to continue to eschew the idea that they have to merely put money into an index fund and leave it there. It's our nature to strive for something more than average.

But that's where it's time to go the other direction. It's possible to set up a portfolio at an extremely low cost these days and maintain it through the use of a suddenly popular product called exchange-traded funds. They provide the possibility of diversification and tax efficiency and the freedom to trade at any point. Now that's a dangerous proposition for some—those of you who have been buying and selling stocks without regard to cost could easily make the same mistake with these products.

Boiling It Down

- Rebalancing has many benefits. It forces discipline as you look at your portfolio a few times a year, and it imposes a strategy that forces you to stick to certain targets instead of letting your emotions get in the way.

- Try to find the lowest-cost solution possible. Some funds do not allow for short-term trading, that is, within 90 days of a purchase. Or use discount brokerages as a method of shifting assets if necessary—remember, the more you trade, the more it costs you.

- Keep it simple: If you do not feel comfortable doing anything more than resetting your assets once a year, stick with that. Even simple rebalancing will help reduce your portfolio's volatility.

- For the more experienced, rebalancing quarterly, or in line with the strategy of certain professionals, may be advisable, but keep the portion used to rebalance based on someone's recommendations limited to only a portion of your portfolio.

Endnotes

[1] Author interview.

[2] Christopher Phillips and Francis Kinniry, "The Active-Passive Debate: Market Cyclicality and Leadership Volatility," Vanguard Investment Counseling and Research, 2009.

[3] Author interview.

[4] Roger Edelen, Richard Evans, and Gregory Kadlec, "Scale Effects in Mutual Fund Performance: The Role of Trading Costs," working paper, March 17, 2007.

[5] Author interview.

[6] Wealth Management Exchange, http://www.wealthmanagementexchange.com/articles/14/1/Managing-Your-Portfolio-Frequent-Rebalancing-Helps-Maintain-Allocation-Targets-/Page1.html.

[7] Yesim Tokat, "Portfolio Rebalancing in Theory and Practice," Vanguard Investment Counseling and Research, May 2007.

[8] Author interview.

[9] Marc J. Trovato, "Diversified Investment Solutions for the New Normal," PIMCO, http://www.pimco.com/LeftNav/Viewpoints/2009/Diversified+Investment+Solutions+by+Trovato+Nov+2009.htm.

[10] Author interview.

[11] Mebane T. Faber, "A Quantitative Approach to Tactical Asset Allocation," *The Journal of Wealth Management*, Spring 2007, updated February 2009.

[12] John Churchill, "Market Timing: Fool's Errand or Prudent Strategy?", *Registered Rep.*, August 2009, http://registeredrep.com/investing/finance-market-timing-0801/index.html.

[13] Daniel Bergstresser, John Chalmers, and Peter Tufano, "Assessing the Costs and Benefits of Brokers in the Mutual Fund Industry," September 26, 2007, published by the Oxford University Press, The Review of Financial Studies.

[14] Author interview.

[15] Marketocracy.com/analysts/topranked.html.

[16] Author interview.

8

ETFs: A Stock By Any Other Name

"I can't help likening the ETF—a cleverly designed financial instrument—to the renowned Purdey shotgun, supposedly the world's best. It's great for big-game hunting in Africa. But it's also great for suicide."
John Bogle, *The Little Book of Common-Sense Investing*

For decades, mutual funds were the asset structure that brought Wall Street home to Main Street. Sure, you could buy individual shares, but many were too frightened to engage in such a game. As a result the mutual fund—where for a fee, a manager bought a basket of stocks hoping to outperform the market—became the investment vehicle of choice for most Americans saving for college or retirement.

Mutual funds are pretty limited in terms of the type of assets they're buying; however, as of December 2009, there were $11.1 trillion in mutual funds, and stock funds accounted for nearly half of that. Money market funds were about $3.2 billion, and bond funds another $2 billion, according to the Investment Company Institute.

With the returns on various stock classes, be it small-cap, emerging market or large-cap, value or growth, increasingly correlated, investors started to look elsewhere for diversification. Interest in commodities, real estate, hedge funds, and gold increased, but some of these investments are notoriously opaque, such as hedge funds. Others, like commodities, present a problem to investors in that the most popular vehicle for investment is futures contracts—where you buy a contract to lock in a particular price on a commodity to be delivered to you a few months or years down the road. But most people really don't want to take delivery of barrels of oil or natural gas (storage would be an issue, unless you've got quite a big shed).

This desire for diversity is, in part, what fueled the growth of the exchange-traded fund (ETF), along with the growing comfort investors have in trading individual shares of stock. ETFs are not stocks, but since they trade on exchanges just as stocks do, they present many of the same characteristics in terms of liquidity and tradability. They've got some distinct advantages, such as tax efficiency, the ability to get in and out whenever you want, and in some cases, super-low expense ratios. However, there's a downside too, particularly for investors without discipline, in that the ability to trade whenever you want can only exacerbate the desire by investors to constantly shift their positions as their emotions take over. From there, all of the same problems that investors have in individual shares rear their ugly heads again—too much trading, which balloons your expenses, and buying and selling at all the wrong times. And some ETFs are just outright perilous for investors, such as leveraged ETFs, which aren't good long-term vehicles.

In recent years, this market has exploded: At the end of 2009 there were nearly 800 different ETFs, with more than 200 broad-based equity funds and nearly 250 global or international ETFs, according to the Investment Company Institute. And while the assets in mutual funds are rising steadily, ETF assets are growing at an even more rapid rate, ending the year at $777.13 billion, a 46 percent increase from the beginning of 2009. Global ETFs nearly doubled in size; bond-focused ETFs had a similar increase. The interest in commodity-oriented ETFs has skyrocketed as well, rising from a mere $32.8 billion at the beginning of 2009 to $74.5 billion at the end of that year.

These asset structures are not without fans, among them prominent investors who are called upon to comment on markets in various publications and on television. Among them is David Kotok, chief investment officer at Vineland, New Jersey-based Cumberland Advisors, who invests solely in ETFs, eschewing individual stock purchases outright. With the tax efficiency and low costs, he values the ability to diversify by sector without having to over-research individual shares, instead concentrating on macroeconomic issues, such as the rise in defense spending that he believes will continue for many years to come. Instead of buying shares in Boeing or Raytheon and thus exposing himself to the vagaries of individual companies, he sticks to defense-oriented ETFs. "In one security, the ETF that has that industry, I have all of the informational advantage that 20 defense analysts have at Goldman Sachs," he says.[1]

Chris Johnson, who runs his own investment strategy practice in Cincinnati, Ohio, concurs, noting that the rise of sector-based ETFs (there are nearly 180 sector-based funds now, not including commodity-focused funds) allows investors to strategize and make picks without bothering with mutual funds that concentrate on such sectors. Since the investments are largely passive (the ETFs are meant to track certain indexes), the costs remain relatively low. "You don't have to worry about management on the fund," he says. "Typically you don't have to worry about fund management altering their performance—you can find the sector you like and group of stocks you like and purchase it."[2]

So should novice investors engage in this kind of back-and-forth activity in specific sector-based ETFs? That's not as easy to determine. It goes back to what I wrote earlier about the ability of investors to gain advantage through buying and selling sectors. Most investors aren't so good at it, and using ETFs doesn't make it any easier (and in fact can help you compound your errors by encouraging you to buy and sell more quickly).

However, the trading costs are starting to diminish, which is a good thing. Charles Schwab & Co. introduced commission-free trading of ETFs in late 2009. Before that, the costs associated with an active back-and-forth strategy from one ETF sector to another made it likely that once again, investors were going to end up eating up their returns with the overhead of trading.

Where ETFs shine is in this instance: When an investor is looking to make one purchase (say, a big rollover of funds from a 401(k) plan to an individual retirement account), and the aim is to sock that purchase away for the long-term, particularly in an account that is subject to taxes. The Standard & Poor's SPDRs ETF—which tracks the S&P 500 index, and is by far one of the largest ETFs in terms of size—comes with a ridiculously low expense ratio of 0.09 percentage point, coming in right at the same level as the likes of Fidelity Spartan and Vanguard's Admiral indexing funds. They're also super-liquid, as the Spiders, as they're colloquially called, and the counterpart that follows the Nasdaq Composite Index, the QQQQs (or the Cubes, as they're referred to), are usually the most actively traded shares on a daily basis in the equity market. These are advantageous for investors who make a yearly contribution to an IRA or limit their activity to occasional or perhaps quarterly rebalancing, as the "bid-ask spread," that is, the difference between what it costs for a buyer and a seller, is a measly penny. (The most active ETFs have very small bid-ask spreads, which is a benefit to investors, particularly those who trade often.)

For those who contribute monthly or biweekly to a retirement account, however, until recently, ETFs had a disadvantage, because you incurred a sales cost with every purchase in the way that you would with buying individual stocks. "A $10 trading cost is going to destroy your returns over the long run," says Scott Burns, head ETF analyst at Morningstar in Chicago. "If you're making small incremental purchases on a monthly basis, the mutual fund is better advantaged. Any time you're putting in $200 a month and taking $10 off the top for trading costs it won't matter whether it's taxable or nontaxable, the tax efficiency (of ETFs) doesn't overcome a 401(k)-style investment plan."[3]

But things are changing. Discount broker Charles Schwab & Co. in November 2009 introduced commission-free trading of ETFs, provided you're trading ETFs offered by Schwab & Co., using a Schwab account. So is this much of a bargain or not? Turns out that yes, this is a pretty good deal: Schwab's biggest ETFs track the Dow Jones U.S. Total Market Index (about 2,500 stocks) and the Dow Jones U.S. Large-Cap Index (about 750 stocks). They carry miniscule expense ratios of 0.08 percent (others, such as the small-cap ETF, are at about 0.15 percent, which is still quite low). That outdoes some of their competitors in certain categories, such as iShares and Vanguard. These ETFs don't track the S&P, but any total market index of about 2,500 stocks is going to capture the upside of index investing anyway. Whether you want to stick with these ETFs instead of the more well-recognized SPDRs is another matter—still, the Dow Jones indexes are hardly esoteric—they're about as diversified as you'd expect something like the SPDRs would be, and while the Total Market Index is not as extensive as, say, the Russell 3000 or the Wilshire 5000, an index that's mimicking the performance of 2,500 stocks is pretty well covered in terms of its scope.

If by opening an account and trading just ETFs, one can eliminate some costs associated with them, so much the better. "It's going to be a real game-changer in the industry," says Burns. "Now you can dollar-cost average ETFs...that's the single biggest drawback with ETFs, the transaction friction." (Dollar cost averaging refers to buying shares in positions that have declined, thus lowering the overall cost for your holding. If you have 20,000 shares of a stock purchased at $20, and the stock drops to $10, and you buy another 20,000 shares, your average cost is now $15 a share, thus lowering the break-even point. Doing this in ETFs that charge commissions would be cost-prohibitive, most likely.) What Burns is referring to when he says "transaction friction" is the steady cost of buying and selling ETFs, which does add up over time. With Schwab eliminating those charges, it becomes much more cost-effective to move in and out of ETFs.

Not long after Schwab's move, Fidelity Investments teamed up with iShares, one of the largest producers of exchange-traded funds, to offer a similar deal as Schwab. Some of the iShares ETFs are designed to mimic the performance of popular indexes created by well-known index companies, including Russell Investments, Dow Jones, and MSCI Barra, and their bond ETFs follow the well-regarded Barclays indexes (formerly Lehman Brothers). Fidelity also undercut Schwab's commission rate for trading other ETFs, offering trades at $7.95 each instead of $8.95 each.

So why are Schwab and Fidelity doing this? One can only imagine this is the kind of ploy that these companies hope will entice investors to open positions in individual stocks or perhaps some of the more well-known ETFs that are not sponsored and consequently don't come commission-free. In fact, when you click on the page on Schwab's Web site devoted to ETFs, there's a little advertisement that offers 150 free trades, along with commission-free trading of Schwab-sponsored ETFs, when you open an account. Free trades are currency, and if you're going to be someone who rebalances twice a year, hell, 150 free trades can last a long time. But what Schwab (and Fidelity) are banking on is the idea that you'll get so enthralled with their technology, their systems, and just trading in general that you'll soon exhaust the freebies and then, voila!—the company has you— and now you're paying the costs of trading just like everyone else. Don't do it! Resist this temptation!

Not everyone, at first blush, has been a big supporter of ETFs. John Bogle of Vanguard takes a more dramatic and alarmist view of ETFs in *The Little Book of Common-Sense Investing*, assuming that those who buy them aren't likely to buy and hold, but instead engage in trading them. That's an understandable view because he's probably right. The SPDRs are most actively traded on a daily basis on the New York Stock Exchange, with average daily volume of 167 million shares for the three-month period ended January 2010. Bogle's disdain for active trading of indexes shows through, when he writes that "the ETF is a fund designed to facilitate trading in its shares, dressed in the guise of the traditional index fund."

This much is true: It does make trading easier, particularly in total market indexes, sectors, and commodities, and it entices people to constantly adjust incrementally. But the associated cost of trading should give the smart investor pause in the first place—*you don't have to trade them willy-nilly*. (And even with Schwab's move, to make the trading in their ETFs free, then you *still* don't have to trade them as if they're baseball cards. You can buy them, hold them with occasional rebalancing, and keep your costs at next-to-nothing!) Bogle even admits that a long-term approach with ETFs is certainly competition for his index fund, saying that all-stock market ETFs present an alternative for long-term investors that will beat the index fund in terms of costs and tax efficiency, "but only when they are bought and held for the long-term." It's good advice—so do that, and don't look back. (If you start to trade ETFs like you're trading stocks, don't be surprised when your performance suffers because of trading costs and also because you start to underperform the market, too. To take such a wild approach would be, truly, to look a gift horse in the mouth.)

Bogle's fear is that ETFs are being used for one thing: Performance chasing. The statistics on turnover suggest he's right—the most popular ETFs sport a turnover ratio of greater than 100 percent and sometimes more than 1000 percent, meaning the average holding period is about a month-and-a-half, a much shorter period than average turnover on the New York Stock Exchange, which is already pretty short. Some of this is due to arbitrage or hedging-related plays by professional managers, who are finding the ETFs a good vehicle for getting in and out of positions. However, it's also due to trading by individuals, something that actions like the ones undertaken by Schwab are likely to only exacerbate. Bogle noted that Don Phillips, managing director at Morningstar, compared ETFs to precision tools, the kind of invention that can do great things for the right user, but considerable damage for those who don't know what they're doing.

Consider, for a moment, the tax advantages of ETFs. Phillips's colleague Scott Burns did a study in 2009 looking at the tax efficiency of ETFs against mutual funds. What makes an ETF superior in this regard is that they don't stick investors in taxable accounts with sudden capital gains distributions the way mutual funds do. He found that of ETFs in a broad range of 27 different indexes (MSCI, S&P, Russell, Nasdaq), just two ETFs had made a capital gains distribution, where the mutual funds had substantial distributions, sometimes up to 5 percent or more of the fund's net asset value.[4] That's money out of your pocket for doing nothing other than buying the fund. "The ETFs smoked 'em," Burns says of mutual funds. "If you own a mutual fund, the fund has accumulated gains from trading activity, and it distributes those gains to you, and if you don't have cash to pay that, you have to sell your fund."

Overall, according to Burns, exchange-traded funds still carry a lower expense ratio than the average mutual fund, but expense ratios for ETFs are rising, in part because of the ongoing introduction of more exotic ETFs that slice and dice sectors into smaller subsectors. They're still a better value at this point, but the addition of targeted ETFs, along with actively managed ETFs, means the gap is narrowing.

These advantages make ETFs a good bet for further growth going forward, but with that, there's caution. After all, if it's easier to buy them and hold them, it's also easier to buy them and sell them at the wrong times, jump into other ones at the wrong time, and make all of the same mistakes one makes with purchases of individual stocks, just on a sector level or subsector level.

The odder the ETF, the higher the likelihood of more hidden costs that come as a result of frequent trading and lack of liquidity. ETFs function by holding shares of all of the companies in a particular index, and at times, big investors can exchange a basket of the underlying holdings for ETFs shares, or vice versa. This helps reduce the gap between the ETF's share price and the net asset value of the ETF (the share price of the ETF that you're buying), but this becomes harder to do when the underlying investments are hard to find and expensive to trade. What happens then is this: The net asset value of the fund diverges from the price of the ETF, and so when you buy that investment, you're paying too much, and when you sell it, you're getting less than the value of the ETF in return. This is in part the cost of doing business in investments that wouldn't have been available for most investors in the first place, but it's also not a reason to trade them frequently. This point is even more important to consider with fixed-income ETFs. With the exception of Treasury bonds, the underlying assets in the growing world of bond ETFs are harder to find and more difficult to price as they don't trade as frequently as, say, the S&P 500 index. The *Wall Street Journal* noted in a March 2010 article that the rush of capital into bond-focused ETFs has exacerbated this tendency for ETFs to trade at premiums to the net asset value of the fund.[5] It's one of the reasons to lean to bond mutual funds rather than ETFs in this area, as bonds are always priced at their net asset value.

As this market has grown, ETFs have become more specialized, developed with the (hopeful) goal of enhancing returns with targeted and/or leveraged bets. One of the more alluring and dangerous subsets of ETFs are the leveraged ETFs, which sound nice in theory, but really aren't going to do what one might think they would at first glance. These ETFs aim to provide double or triple the returns of a particular benchmark—or attempt to double or triple the return of a short position (that's a bet on the market falling) in that particular index. But these exchange-traded funds are highly deceptive in terms of what one might expect: Double-long or double-short ETFs are trying to achieve double the returns *every single day*, not on an annual or quarterly basis. Due to the compounding of daily returns, the result is often vastly different than the underlying index. So if the S&P gains 2 percent on one day, the double-long ETFs look to gain 4 percent that day. But this does not mean if the S&P goes up 20 percent in a year, the double-ETF goes up 40 percent!

Case in point: In 2009, the Standard & Poor's 500-stock index posted a total return of 26.5 percent. ProShares Ultra S&P 500, which tries to double the index, gained 46 percent, which falls short of doubling the index (remove the 0.95 percentage point expense ratio, and it's still not quite double the index). An even better example would be to look at the difference between the Dow Jones U.S. Financials Index, which rose nearly 17 percent in 2009. Now compare that to the ProShares Ultra Financials, which aims to double the daily return of the DJ financial index. Did it gain 34 percent? Hardly—the ETF *lost* 5.4 percent in 2009. The UltraShort Financials ETF—which is trying to double the opposite of the Dow Jones U.S. Financials Index—was horrific, losing nearly 77 percent in 2009.[6] That's a perfect storm of leverage and instability for you, and it's something to stay away from.

Managed ETFs and Other Wrinkles

Growth in ETFs appears likely to come from several places. Sector or country-specific ETFs and actively managed ETFs are likely to continue to be a growth area, along with perhaps a combination of the two (an actively managed ETF focusing on small-cap stocks, for instance). The most popular sector ETFs are in natural resources and technology, although State Street, which sponsors the SPDRs ETF, has S&P sector ETFs for nine of the ten S&P sectors (telecommunications is the lone exception—it's folded into another area); new ones continue to crop up. For professional investors attempting to beat the market, they're an ideal vehicle because they carry a relatively low cost and have tax efficiency, as Kotok of Cumberland Advisors has pointed out. But Bogle quoted (anonymously) a chief investment officer at an ETF company cautioning against "pin-pointed" bets on sectors, because they "still involve nearly as much risk as concentrated stock picks." But that doesn't mean they're going to stop growing. Like mutual funds, tech stocks, tech funds, and other hot investments that dominated the landscape for a time, the ETF world is turning into its own "app economy," as Nicholas Colas, chief market strategist at BNY ConvergEx Group, puts it. This, by itself, is not necessarily a bad thing, but with more choices comes more confusion.

Another area where one can expect a growth spurt is in actively managed ETFs, first introduced by investor Harry Dent with his Dent Fund (ticker symbol: DENT) through AdvisorShares, which is now marketing other new actively managed exchange-traded funds. And so ETFs are starting to come full circle: While this is still designed for the same kind of tax efficiency and liquidity offered as most ETFs, now investors have the (supposed) benefit of active management—but the higher expenses to boot. Dent's fund carries an expense ratio of 1.56 percent, and if such a ratio becomes the norm with active ETFs, the low-cost advantages of the structure are suddenly out the window.[7] Part of the fund's expense ratio includes a 0.17 percentage point expense for the cost of holding other ETFs—those ETFs you could just buy on your own, particularly the index ETFs, which carry half the cost of this small component of the overall expense! And if the ETF doesn't perform well, then what? That tax efficiency isn't all that helpful with fund costs eating up returns in the first place.

Actively managed ETFs at this point are still in their infancy—but State Street, which produces the SPDRs, has already filed with regulators for the opening of an actively managed ETF, and they're not alone; other major fund companies have done the same thing. Naturally, though, providers of ETFs are concerned that there's no track record for fund managers who would actively manage ETFs. John Gabriel, another Morningstar analyst, says this structure may take off once a prominent fund manager decides to start managing an ETF. The other option fund companies have is to convert an existing mutual fund into an ETF structure, which would allow intraday trading, better tax treatment, and more liquidity, and from there, it would have an established track record as well. Of course, this doesn't help you if you're stuck with an ETF, once a mutual fund, which had a strong record of returns before you bought it, only to see the thing tank when you buy into it.

The rise of active management of ETFs also garners this question: What if there's a run on an ETF? An actively managed ETF is only as good as its holdings, and at a time when professional investors are looking to game the market as much as possible, it won't be long before there's a cottage industry of people who pore over the published holdings of actively managed ETFs and find those with the most problematic portfolios. Now, that exchange traded fund's holdings may have changed if quarterly data is all that's available, but markets have moved quickly before on less information—talk of hedge-fund redemptions is enough to send investors flocking out of vehicles that are much harder to abandon than something like an ETF. What happens if a fund is discovered to have had two or three holdings that are suddenly blowing up? Investors will start selling indiscriminately, and unlike the sector ETF, which is going to go down or up based on fundamentals of the underlying sector, rumors may be enough to hit these ETFs hard. By contrast, runs on a mutual fund are more difficult. (To be sure, Gabriel of Morningstar says a run is unlikely, but statements like that have been made about other products before.)

With about 800 ETFs in existence now, there does not seem to be a limit to the number of flavors that can be invented. By no means is the ETF world anywhere near close to saturation, but the growth area would seem to have to be in actively managed ETFs. Once that novelty has worn off, though, investors will find they're buying another mutual fund. Sure, a more tax-efficient and liquid mutual fund, but a fund just the same, and investors are back to the same story: Reduce costs and buy the market, or try to chase performance and see how it all works out.

Since ETFs have grown in popularity, particularly ETFs that track assets other than stocks and bonds, it's time to look at a few of the other asset classes that are likely to provide good diversification if they're part of your portfolio. Some of them are undeniably safer than stocks, but don't have the potential of equities. Others are more volatile, but thankfully tend to move differently than stocks. With the right allocation, they're good offsets to the volatile nature of stocks and the growing correlation between domestic and international stocks. But with many of these asset classes, the popular presentation is meant to entice you to do all of the wrong things you've done with the stock market, too.

Boiling It Down

- ETFs are a great vehicle for quickly building a diversified portfolio in many assets, including stocks, bonds, commodities, and currencies.
- Take advantage of low-cost offers of free trading in ETFs to set up portfolios and to rebalance.
- Consider using ETFs for a big buy-and-hold purchase, such as an IRA rollover.
- Resist the temptation to trade frequently, no matter how many free trades you're given—they will eventually run out.
- Treat actively managed ETFs the way you would an actively managed mutual fund: Look at the costs involved. Is there a cheaper option? Is there an advantage? More than likely, there probably is not.

Endnotes

[1] Author interview.

[2] Author interview.

[3] Author interview.

[4] Scott Burns, "ETFs Deliver on Their Tax-Efficiency Promise," May 19, 2009, http://news.morningstar.com/articlenet/article.aspx?id=292280.

[5]Sam Mamudi, "Bond ETF Buyers Must Stay on Guard for Hidden Risks," *Wall Street Journal*, March 1, 2010.

[6]Performance data from company Web sites.

[7]Fund company prospectus.

9

Crude and Rude: Commodities, Bonds, and Everything Else You Should (and Shouldn't) Buy

"[Gold] gets dug out of the ground in Africa, or someplace.
Then we melt it down, dig another hole, bury it again and pay
people to stand around guarding it. It has no utility. Anyone
watching from Mars would be scratching their head."
Warren Buffett, 1988

When people forget the past, they're doomed to repeat it. In financial markets, they repeat it with other asset classes.

Amid the stock market turmoil of 2008, commercials began appearing on CNBC for brokerage Lind-Waldock. "Bought the wrong stock again," a sad, morose looking guy says to a friend. She advises him to invest in commodities. He moans something along the lines of, "What do I know about pork bellies?" but she sets him straight, telling him to trade what he knows: "You know crude oil, right? Gold? With commodities there's no P/E ratios or CEO scandals—it's a pure price play." A later commercial brings in a smug guy who asks his dopey buddy, "You're still trading stocks?" Maybe that's a legit question but he obviously advises his friend to trade commodities, not back off and just stick with long-term investments.

People are gun-shy when bitten, so they usually don't make the same mistakes with something that's lost them money. Often, though, they perceive the problem to be with the underlying investment and not the action they're taking. So mistakes are made again, and commodities are a recent fad.

With growing interest in oil, gold, and other commodities, and easier facilitation for investing in these asset classes through lower account minimums or, more importantly, exchange-traded funds, suddenly the idea of investing in energy and metals, emerging markets, hedge funds, real estate, and all sorts of other assets outside of bonds and stocks has become a reality for individuals. With that came, of course, the marketing campaign, such as the one Lind-Waldock settled on, where the essential message was: "Investing is still easy— you're just buying the wrong stuff! Instead, buy our product, because we know better!" The advertisements in question play to both the vanity of the individual investor and attempt to flatter you, putting forth the idea that yes, you know what you're doing, but you just got screwed by those other guys. In addition, buying this asset class is easier than the other one—no fundamentals, just prices! Just things that go up! The tone is reminiscent of George Carlin's comedic routine about the difference between the endlessly complex game of football and the blindingly silly game of baseball, where the only objective is to "go home. I'm going home! Wheeee!" This is sort of like that. "Prices go up, and that's good! Yay!" You feel empowered by this commercial—after all, you're an investor, so this should be easy, right?

And with that, the practice of cajoling investors into seemingly simple decisions asserts itself again. Commodities have become a popular alternative investment category because they're one of the few that have emerged in recent years that truly qualifies as another asset, unlike hedge funds (which are just investment vehicles buying other things) or funds-of-funds (same thing). There are a number of raw materials that have been consistently strong performers over the recent years, but what's more important is that they have generally showed a low correlation with stocks or bonds, which again means that they're going to go a different direction than stocks or bonds.

Professional investors have mixed views regarding the benefits of you or me investing in hard assets. On the one hand, they are notoriously volatile, prone to slipping into sharp bear markets without warning. However, they are generally less correlated with assets such as stocks. The GLD ETF sports a rolling three-month correlation with the S&P 500 tracking ETF of about 0.5, which shows it has had a reasonably solid relationship, but hardly moves in lockstep.[1] Historically, the asset correlation has been much lower, but it has increased in the last two years or so as monetary policy officials flooded markets with liquidity that has seemed to find its way into just about every financial asset. Oil historically held a relatively low correlation with stocks, but that relationship has become rather strong since the onset of the financial crisis in late 2008, and it has remained tethered to stocks since. It's more than likely to separate at some point, but it's unclear when.

It has not gone unnoticed by the mass investing public. The U.S. Oil Trust exchange-traded fund, which is run by Brown Brothers Harriman, was created in April 2006 as the price of crude oil rose to $70 a barrel. It eventually peaked at about $150 a barrel in the summer of 2008 when the rest of the world looked to be falling apart, and since then it's been crushed, lately trading pretty much around the same levels as when the USO started. The fund has grown to about $1.68 billion in assets as of late April 2010.[2] Perhaps the USO is a great way to get exposure to the oil markets, but even those who got in at the beginning are taking it on the chin—at the end of 2009, the fund was down 41.7 percent since inception.

The USO ETF and similar products that track other funds also differ from stock or bond-based ETFs; in the USO, the investor owns the one-month futures contract, making ownership somewhat of a bet on commodities futures rather than the actual underlying product. And the weird gyrations that can take place in that market make it more difficult for investors to understand, says Scott Burns of Morningstar. "It's based on a futures/derivatives-type strategy and that's what people don't understand," he says.

The appeal of oil is easy to see: For a long time, individual investors were basically limited to stocks, bonds, or cash, or investing structures that invested in those three (and perhaps real estate). That's not the case anymore. And while Lind-Waldock might want to suggest that the "pure price play" appeal of buying oil or natural gas or wheat futures makes it easier to do than buying stock, the reality is that those markets are prone to big shocks at random moments, particularly the less liquid ones, which is basically any commodity outside of oil, gold, silver, and a few other fuel markets. "There are so many exogenous events or factors that impact oil, and if you're not looking at it every day and you miss something you could eviscerate 50 percent of your portfolio in a week if you're levered," says Chris Edmonds, who invests in commodities at FIG Partners in Atlanta.[3]

When it comes to popular commodity-related ETFs, though, the USO has nothing on the SPDR Gold Shares ETF, which tracks the price of gold and trades under the symbol GLD. If there's any one ETF that is ripe for speculating, it's this one, thanks to recent trends in the gold market. Investors rushed headlong into gold in the latter part of the decade, owing to several factors. One was the asset's status as a safe haven in times of trouble. Another was the devaluation of currencies worldwide, which enhanced the appeal of a precious metal that has value in just about any country. And third, the simmering conspiracy theories about the end of the world sparked more interest in this "end of days" asset. Gold has certainly been on a tear—after years of fetching barely $200 an ounce, it has traded between $750 and $1100 an ounce for the better part of five years, owing mostly to increased speculative activity in the asset thanks to the growth of ETFs—the GLD in particular.

This ETF first showed up on the New York Stock Exchange in 2004, and was worth nearly $40 billion as of mid-February 2010 and traded on several exchanges. What's more, it was the second-largest ETF in the world, trailing only the S&P Select SPDRs, which tracks the broad S&P 500 index.

Gold, in many ways, is the perfect example of the "plausible fad" that we associate with the ballyhooed promotion of the Nifty Fifty, the Dogs of the Dow, or other seemingly safe-but-risky investments. After all, gold actually does exist, and for years has been considered the ultimate expression of safety because it is assumed that in some sort of massive breakdown in modern economic society, gold, prized by many, would retain value for people when their banknotes suddenly were determined to be worthless. And there is an element of truth to that—from a theoretical perspective. The reality is, we're so far from a breakdown to a barter-based economy that such discussions are foolish. Unfortunately, gold only has value because we as a general public say it has value—in the same way salt was once a valued and rare commodity. It does not have the industrial uses as do silver or platinum, never mind a more practical metal such as copper. In 2007, there were about 3,500 tons in identifiable demand, and more than 2,400 tons were used for jewelry and another 650 tons were used in "retail investment," which means hoarding of bars or through ETFs, leaving about 450 tons used in electronics, dentistry, and other applications.

So most gold is used more or less for shiny objects, which is great, but cannot form the backbone of an investment strategy. (Tell this to a die-hard gold fanatic, and you'll get a treatise on why gold is being systematically undervalued by world governments as a result of some sort of worldwide plot. You have better things to do than to listen to such nonsense.)

More evidence of gold's status as the current plausible fad is the recent surge in advertisements from outfits nobody's heard of suggesting people either start hoarding the stuff or selling it off for a great price. That does not speak well to its fundamentals. For instance, former baseball player Keith Hernandez may be a heck of a person, but what is he doing endorsing companies that buy or sell gold from retail customers? "When people make too big of a deal of certain things, you know there's something wrong with it," Edmonds says. "All these ads started popping up for the firms that trade gold—why did that happen?

There's a lot of momentum, and a lot of people talking about gold, and it could sucker a lot of people into it. You don't see IBM advertising, telling people to buy their stock."

The vaunted gold ETF has problems of its own that other ETFs do not, however. The tax rate for sales of long-term holdings of what's known as "collectibles" is a hefty 28 percent instead of 15 percent for long-term capital gains, and you can get socked with that if you unload some of your ETF holdings that are in a taxable account (obviously a 401(k) plan is treated differently). "For regular accounts, for most investors, you want to stay away from the bullion ETF, whether it's silver or gold," says Thomas Winmill, president of Midas Management, which invests in metals and metals companies. Winmill's a big metals guy, investing heavily in hard assets and mining companies, but he's wary of investors putting their money in the asset class, figuring that many people who have real estate—that is, own a home— probably could live without hard assets like gold or silver. Those who rent, however, could probably afford to put 10 percent of their money in hard assets, although he tends to argue for mining company stocks (or in your case, an ETF), because the operating leverage of companies that mine gold, silver, or platinum means that when prices go up, their stocks will probably rise much more than that.

He believes the more natural time to invest in hard assets is when so-called "real" interest rates are negative, or headed in that direction thanks to rising inflation rates.[4] Real rates are calculated by taking the benchmark bond rate—say, the ten-year yield—and subtracting the rate of inflation. As of early 2010, inflation was running at about 3 percent, and the ten-year was trading around 3.7 percent, leaving a meager 0.70 percentage point real rate. With inflation likely to head higher, the real rate will remain low or perhaps continue to diminish. As a result, bonds are losing money to inflation, making a hard asset that appreciates in price more valuable for the time being.

Regardless of this, commodities are definitely one of a few "other" assets outside stocks and bonds that represent a different asset class, and are generally uncorrelated enough to be worth one's investment. When it comes to diversification, we've already talked about how other asset classes formerly went their own way, but have been tethered to the stock market in the last several years amid the ongoing boom-bust cycle. That does not mean emerging markets stocks, foreign stocks, international debt, or currency investments are suddenly not worth it because they have become more closely aligned with the U.S. markets. But they also don't represent something fundamentally different.

Other Asset Classes

I would be remiss to not mention some of the other major assets that have emerged as investment possibilities. So what qualifies as another "asset class"? It has to be an end investment and not just an investment vehicle. Stocks are an asset class, and one can plausibly say that emerging market stocks can be considered separate from developed country stocks; the same goes with government debt, corporate debt, and emerging-market debt.

Real estate is certainly an asset class that has its advantages and disadvantages. It, too, appreciates more dramatically during times of price inflation. Whereas stocks are thought of as a decent way to protect one's portfolio against inflation, the individual actions of corporate managers and growth trends for specific companies are part of the fundamental equation. Assuming a property is kept in good shape, it will generally rise with the fortunes of similar properties in well-located areas. The reality for many investors, however, is you can overdo it in real estate if you already own a home, tying much of your fortune to how the real estate market does if you eventually decide to sell your own dwelling. Additional investments in real estate will tether you even more to the real estate markets.

It's worth dispensing with a couple of investments that aren't worth as much time for investors because they're really not asset classes, just investment vehicles that are buying other assets. If you're rich enough to afford the management fees of a top hedge fund manager, you're probably not reading this book anyway, but if you are, best of luck to you. Everyone else is not going to have the kind of capital available to really take advantage of a hedge fund, so you're just buying management costs that will dilute your investment. With that in mind, anything that advertises itself as a "fund of funds" is something to be wary of—after all, it's a fund (which charges you money) investing in funds (which charge money too), and if you're being sold this by a brokerage, there's another fee also. By the time you've gotten to invest anything, you're already substantially in the hole.

Bond. Treasury Bond.

The next most popular investment and often a primary component in a portfolio after stocks are bonds, for good reason. They're guaranteed to return your principal if that's your intention, with a (relatively small) return from the interest you get for owning the fixed income asset. Bond portfolios can also be constructed through direct purchases from the U.S. Treasury, which you can use to create what's known as a "laddered" portfolio consisting of bonds of different maturities to help protect you against rising rates.

Bonds of differing maturities can also be looked at as distinct— short-term debt such as Treasury bills have certain advantages that long-term debt does not (because it matures more frequently), but also has disadvantages (generally, it is very low-yielding paper). And bonds are going to remain one of the more important asset classes in the average person's portfolio, because they're designed to return one's capital rather than open it up to the possibility of outright losses.

As stated previously, the bond market had a nice run for, oh, the last 40 years or so, managing to outdo the stock market thanks to a horrific run for equities in the first decade of the nascent 21st century.

Many investments were beneficiaries of the sharp decline in inflation that began in the early 1980s thanks to the policies of Federal Reserve chairman Paul Volcker, but corporate, high-yield, and government debt did especially nicely. With yields having reached historic lows in the last few years, the prospect of another two-decade run in bonds is slim. That doesn't mean they don't have some value as an investment—they do—but they're not going to outperform.

Investors have gotten used to thinking of debt mostly in terms of the Treasury's long-term obligations, ten-year notes and 30-year notes, which it issues to cover payments for government spending. But the Treasury sells a ton of short-term obligations—bills with maturities of 30 days, or 90 days, or six months, and one advantage to debt of this type is that in an environment where the economy begins to recover and inflation starts to rise, this debt will respond more favorably than long-term debt. Since long-term bonds mature several years down the line, a five-year note that carries a yield of just 3 percent is going to be an unfavorable investment if inflation rises to 3 percent or more—in fact, that five-year note is losing value. Now, all debt loses value when inflation is rising. Stocks are in some ways a better investment as the underlying company can respond to inflation by raising prices and therefore potentially earning more money (and stock prices, if they appreciate fast enough, can outrun inflation). But if there's one type of debt that's going to recover its value more quickly, it's short-term debt—that is, certificates of deposit and money market funds.

When inflation rises, current investments lose their value. Throwing one dollar into a drawer for a year in a 3 percent inflation environment puts you in a situation where a $1 purchase in January would cost $1.03 in December—but your dollar is still just one dollar. And so it is with debt as well. The difference is that short-term CD rates can adjust pretty quickly to respond to rising inflation, and money market funds become immediately more attractive. So your holdings are still going to lose money on a relative basis with inflation rising, but not as much as long-term debt. "Anything in a rising interest rate environment is going to take a hit, but money markets are liable to start paying the best rates the quickest," says David John Marotta. "The biggest advantage is that it does not go down in a rising interest rate environment and starts paying higher interest almost immediately."

On some level, this is not an issue if you are what's known as a "coupon clipper." That is, you buy a bond for the coupon—a 5 percent bond, for instance, is going to give you 5 percent every year, and then at the end of five years, you get your money back. That's a guarantee from the government and corporate issuers (although the risk of loss is higher with corporate issues). If you're buying bonds directly from the U.S. Treasury (a nice, low-cost way of going about putting together a fixed-income portfolio), you can get the interest rate you want without worrying about losing principal. However, if you're invested in a bond fund that is more than likely trading that debt back and forth, the chances of losing money increase with the prospect of rising inflation and falling debt prices. "If you need to sell [a longer term bond] you'll take a loss on it," Marotta says. "And if you had cash, you could get more for it anyway."

There is another option available for investors: Treasury inflation protected securities, or TIPs. The value of these securities rises when inflation goes up, and so they're designed to be a hedge against rising inflation. If the rate of inflation remains stagnant, there won't be much of an additional return, but they're a nice way to fill out the portfolio; they hedge against those investments that are going to definitely lose ground when inflation rises (such as cash, long-term debt, and a number of other kinds of bonds, as well as certain stocks), but they're not going to suck away your returns in a strong environment for everything else. More companies are starting to respond to investor desire for something that protects them against inflation— American Century Investments recently announced the launch of a fund designed to protect against rising prices through buying TIPs along with certain stock classes and commodities.

I'm not aiming to go through every asset class for its positive and negative points, but one thing that investors should keep in mind in coming years is that unlike the early 1980s, when stocks and bonds were undervalued, or the early 1990s, when commodities and real estate were trading at discounts to historical value, the new decade has begun with many major asset classes trading at levels that can, at best, be considered fair value, but are more likely than not expensive when compared with historic trends. Stocks cheapened considerably in the 2008-2009 blowup, but with a 75 percent rally since, most of the bargains have been easily had. Bonds continue to yield very little, and some decline in prices is going to occur. Gold hasn't been this valuable in three decades, and oil may not be at $150 a barrel anymore, but that doesn't mean it's cheap, either. Corporate and high yield debt also slipped in 2008, eventually trading at a bargain, but those assets rebounded in the great 2009 rally as well. Emerging markets are no longer as inefficiently valued, and many markets, such as China, Brazil, and India, are in the midst of bull runs that may last for a number of years—or could be interrupted by fallow periods lasting a few years as well. Real estate is coming off its most overvalued period in decades in the U.S., and that goes both for residential and commercial real estate properties; they're all in a long, multiyear declining process. So what is cheap? Troubled companies and countries that are in danger of defaulting on their debt obligations—but they're cheap for a reason. And cash, one supposes, but leaving it under the mattress isn't any kind of strategy.

This chapter isn't meant to scare you out of investing entirely. After all, it would be pretty ridiculous to claim that you shouldn't buy stocks, and, oh, don't buy anything else either. The fact is that to garner strong returns and still sleep at night, you have to diversify, and that may mean buying a number of already-expensive assets. However, not all of them will be pricey at once, and keeping a relatively balanced allocation to all of them will mitigate losses from those that fall short of expectations. We've already discussed how diversity doesn't always save the day, but that's in part because of ineffective diversification—divvying up your money into two asset classes (stocks and bonds) and then further into various subsets of the first one (stocks) isn't enough, not when commodities, real estate, other types of corporate debt, and short-term debt are available.

It's also because you and I aren't proactive enough with our own investments, sticking to certain allocations and failing to alter them in any way. What the next several years are going to require is twofold: flexibility and an eye towards your costs of investment. There's no such thing as a free lunch, but in a more regulated financial services industry that's struggling to rebound from the go-go 1990s and early 2000s, there's going to be certain bargains and ways to cut your costs. Some of these ideas are pretty rudimentary, and others were happened upon, but they're all pretty simple to implement. Amid that it's time also to get to the checklist—the list of things you need to do to put together a relatively well-balanced, diversified portfolio that you can rebalance on a periodic basis.

Boiling It Down

- Your portfolio isn't complete without bonds. They're not a panacea, but they do provide some diversification and reduce risk.
- Treasury inflation protected securities (TIPs) can help keep up with inflation.
- Consider adding some commodities to your portfolio, but be forewarned: They aren't cheap, and the funds that invest in them often carry high costs as well.

Endnotes

[1] Assetcorrelation.com.

[2] United States Oil Fund, http://www.unitedstatesoilfund.com/uso-holdings.php.

[3] Author interview.

[4] Author interview.

10

Putting It All Together

"Everybody needs money. That's why they call it money."
Danny DeVito, *Heist*

One of my most important lessons learned about finances came—repeatedly—via my mother's lengthy and irate telephone conversations with whatever insurance company or brokerage representative was unfortunate enough to answer when it was her turn in the customer service queue. My mother is not the world's most sophisticated investor when it comes to asset allocation, but when it came to disputed charges on accounts—any account at all—she had one easy rule: Never pay. *"Don't ever pay. Ever,"* she told me once, soon after letting the poor sap on the other side of the phone call know this exact fact. The advice stuck—even though it had to be repeated to me on occasion when I thought resolution was the better path to take through first paying a bill and then attempting to work out whether I should in fact send the check or not. This doesn't mean she was a scofflaw of some kind; she did and still does meet her obligations. But in a dispute, she doesn't lay out one red cent until the problem is satisfactorily resolved.

It's easy to take that lesson and apply it entirely to investing. Just ask yourself—is this worth the money I'm paying? There are plenty of investment opportunities that involve hefty sales charges and big expenses, and offers of advice that aren't much more than a computer simulation and a lot of marketing material. If you don't have to pay for it, *don't*. At some point, you will have to pay for something—be it a transaction fee, 12b-1 fee, management charges in a mutual fund—but without a doubt, every charge should be scrutinized, even if it ends up costing you 15 minutes on the phone with someone from the financial services industry. (I can attempt to get my mother to wear them down first if need be.)

The essential point here that I'm getting at is that having cash is not a terrible thing. A bit of extra money that comes as the result of saving on a weekly basis, scrimping on fees by purchasing funds on a commission-free basis, or maxing out the employer's 401(k) match, cannot be ignored. If someone is going to give you something for free, take it. The old adage is that there's no such thing as a free lunch, but some things can be basically cost-free if you're disciplined enough not to give in and merely "start paying."

Let's just start with cash in general, and with the easiest ways to preserve your capital, and then we'll get into ways to reduce your overall costs. Let's start with forced savings. This isn't a book about how to start saving, so I'm going to keep this bit short, but there isn't a bank these days that doesn't have options in its online banking services to create automatic transfers to a savings or money market account. So start with $20 a week or a bit more, if you're not already. I can already hear people howling about not having the money to afford this, but the reality is, you can't afford not to do this.

The forced savings is a greater benefit than you realize: It helps you save, but it also engenders a bit of frugality, which can come in handy if you need to reduce your expenses. From here, you can set a goal—each time $1,000 or say $3,000 is accumulated, you can then move that to some kind of individual retirement account, or make a once a year contribution that gets invested in the lowest-cost asset you can find.

Cash is the easiest, most liquid instrument to have, so if there is a sudden desire or need to increase the risk in your portfolio, well, you have the assets available. Furthermore, everyone's needs for retirement change over time, and there are going to be times when you need to save more, and times you need to save less.

One other way to generate more free cash is to limit your obligations—particularly debts, and specifically credit card debt. Without existing balances, your cash is free to be used for savings and investment. Your balances have to be paid off monthly, so that debt needs to be wound down because those high interest rates cannot be made up with the returns you'll get on investment.

Nothing Is Free; Some Things Come Close

Now that you're saving, we come to the more interesting stuff. Yes, there's no such thing as a free lunch and what not, but when something is offered free, take it. Here are a few examples of such.

Many people with full-time jobs participate in a 401(k) plan. This is a nice investment vehicle—it doesn't have the intermediary of a brokerage to take away more fees from you, the assets can be shifted without tax consequences, and there's the tax benefit because it reduces your taxable income. Investing in a 401(k) is, by now, a no-brainer. If you can't maximize your contributions, and many people find it difficult to do so, you'd better put in at least to the maximum of what your company will match. Many people say it's necessary to save at least 10 percent of your income a year. But if you've got a lot of obligations thanks to growing children or saving for college accounts, and your company will match up to, say, 4 percent, well, then you can contribute 6 percent and let your company add in 4 more, and you've got 10 percent. Most companies have a vesting schedule when it comes to 401(k) matches, but unless it's a rolling schedule (where you always have at least 20 to 25 percent that won't be considered vested), soon you'll be vested, the money will be yours, and that'll boost your retirement assets.

Second, as we talked about earlier, commission-free trading of ETFs—and free trades for those who open accounts at various discount brokerages—should be taken advantage of as long as there are no strings attached that mandate a certain number of trades per year. If Schwab or someone else is going to let you trade ETFs without any additional burdens in terms of having to trade, well, that's something for free—take it and dole those out at an extremely stingy rate, making just a trade or two a year to rebalance or add an asset class as more ETFs become available, and that's it. (Schwab's pricing guide, available online, does not show any restrictions for trading ETFs. In addition, they also don't charge a commission for trades of Treasury bills, notes, bonds, and TIPs, making it easier to build a portfolio of bonds as well.) The extreme cheapness of these ETFs will make building the stocks portion of your portfolio a snap, and the 401(k) plan, if it has a lot of options, will enable you to put together the fixed-income proportion of your portfolio relatively easily. From there, finding products to take the commodities and inflation-protection portion of the portfolio might be a bit more difficult and will probably cost more, but if you're offsetting that with minimal costs for the stocks and bonds, you can afford to pay a little more for the more esoteric assets. Finally, short-term obligations like CDs and Treasury bills are also cheap (and easy to roll over), so the expenses there will remain low.

Now we come to the rebalancing portion: This is going to cost money if you're doing it too frequently (so don't), and it's going to bite if you're doing it in taxable accounts, such as vehicles that are not specifically designed for retirement. So the way to hold costs down is to rebalance your portfolio, but rebalance in the nontaxed areas such as your 401(k) plan or individual retirement accounts, and use the other accounts to hold a steady proportion of your assets in one or two types of asset classes.

Let's say, for instance, you've got a million dollars in investments (we should all be so lucky) and you want to maintain, very basically, a 60-40 split between stocks and bonds. We've already said this split isn't optimum because it's not diversified enough, but for this example let's just go with it. If you've got a $700,000 401(k) account and a taxable account with a $300,000 balance, move all of the latter into the bond market. This way, you've got 30 percent in bonds, and the 401(k) account, which has another 70 percent of your assets, can be split so you have an additional 10 percent of your total in bonds, and the rest in equities. If the stock market outperforms, moving the overall allocation to about 65-35, all you need to do is sell the stock and rebalance in the 401(k) account and leave the other account alone. You're still balanced effectively because of your overall allocation—even if one taxable account is concentrated in one type of investment.

We've already discussed the need to rebalance your portfolio, but you want to do it at an optimal cost, of course. In a 401(k) plan or IRA account, this is easier, but the aim is to limit the number of trades you make a year. Returns tend to be stronger for those who rebalance quarterly, and trading in ETFs should allow you to do that without too much incremental pain, but you can also elect to do it a bit less, say, twice a year. In addition, if you're going to be occasionally buying and selling ETFs, you are electing to trade in the market (unlike a mutual fund, where you just get the closing price), and if that's the case, another cost-saving move is to stick only to limit orders, not market orders. With a limit order, you dictate the price you want to get when you sell an asset—with a market order, you're at the mercy of those doing the trading, and they don't give a darn what the price is for you. So whatever price you want, that's the one you ask for, using a limit order. This advice is generally geared more to those who are actually buying stocks, but it comes into play in ETFs as well.

In general, though, you want to limit your trading, particularly in the types of assets (like small-cap and international ETFs, along with any ETF that buys bonds other than government debt or debt sold by Fannie Mae and Freddie Mac) where the pricing and the liquidity aren't as good as large-cap and total market ETFs. Bonds don't trade as much as stocks, and they're harder for investment management companies to find, thus making the cost greater, and that cost will transfer to you, which saps your total returns.

That's not to say, however, that you shouldn't ever consider making sales of your assets—those in taxable accounts, that is (rebalancing in tax-advantaged accounts is of course easy). Many advisors note that clients lost money over the years, especially as the market started to head south, because they were afraid to sell their holdings and thus incur a taxable event because they didn't want to be forced into laying out funds for taxes. But everybody has to pay taxes! Capital gains are definitely not free, and I don't know how you feel, but I'd much rather pay capital gains on an investment that netted a 30 percent gain than elect not to sell anything and then incur an outright loss of 20 percent that didn't have to happen because you were afraid of selling your assets. In fact, this is a good time to return to the subject mentioned earlier—the countless stories I've heard from individuals who lost money in part because they were talked out of it by financial advisors who counseled against selling shares and instead told them the brief declines were just that—brief. That's where discipline comes in; in addition to rebalancing every year or twice a year or at whatever interval, you don't need to be afraid to sell assets that aren't working at a particular time. Most stock markets in the last century have at one point or another lost 50 to 75 percent of their value, but there's no reason you need to be a part of that.

We've already talked about the 200-day moving average phenomena—the strategy devised by Mebane Faber to sell your stocks if the S&P 500 moves below its 200-day moving average and buy back when it goes back above. A simpler way to go is to put in, for instance, stop losses at about 15 percent if a certain asset should lose that much money. A stop loss is a direct order to your broker that requires them to sell your assets after a certain amount of losses. Theoretically, if the stock market continues to fall, you've at least gotten yourself out in time to avoid more losses; this would have worked with the big plunge in oil after it peaked in 2008, and the same for stocks as well in

2008. The primary question becomes, of course, when to get back in. That's a harder one to answer. Many investors would choose not to return to the market for a lengthy period of time, often until stocks have rallied substantially, and by then, they've given up significant gains they could have had if they'd maintained an allocation in the market.

Stop loss strategies help mitigate the human nature to let losses continue to build up, but there are some inefficiencies, as Adam Lei and Huihua Li pointed out in the *Financial Services Review* in 2009. The problem is this: They don't necessarily improve returns, because long-run buy-and-hold strategies can overcome the benefit of stop losses. So what's the point? They can on some levels reduce your risk by providing investors "with disciplines and the potential to reduce investment risk."[1] That means, essentially, that you won't necessarily make your returns better, but you will be consciously deciding that there's a certain amount of pain you're willing to take in a particular investment and no more—and it eliminates the subjective that is so often based on emotions. Plenty of investors have seen their portfolios destroyed as a result of believing the market is "just going to come back," and vainly hang onto their assets without considering that there's nothing heroic about keeping your money in stocks, commodities, or other assets when they're losing value.

There's an adage on Wall Street that your "first loss is your best loss," and while most hackneyed clichés are hackneyed for a reason, this one actually is based on common sense: Selling underperforming assets after they lose at most 10 to 15 percent keeps you from compounding mistakes. If you're so sure something will rebound later on, by all means, buy it back, but only if it loses another 10 or 15 percent. You might also be asking, in a portfolio that has about half the money in equities, does that mean I have to sell all of my stocks whenever it loses 15 percent? No—paring back your holdings will help you remain invested in case the market turns around, but you've also bought yourself, for the time being, an extra bit of cushion against further losses by diversifying into more conservative options.

There are two basic kinds of stop loss strategies. One of them is a straightforward one, where the moment you sell is the same, no matter what, and the other is a "trailing" stop loss, where the sell point comes as the asset price continues to rise. (It does not adjust lower if the stock falls.) Investors generally don't employ these kinds of strategies when they solely invested in mutual funds—they're more used for individual share purchases—but there can be a benefit when it comes to exchange-traded funds, because it enforces a discipline, forcing investors to move to bonds or cash when the asset in question declines precipitously.

"Because a stop loss strategy allows the sale of a security to be automatic when the security price drops, this feature can possibly prevent investors from behavioral biases that may otherwise cause them to hold their losing investments too long," Lei and Lei wrote.

What Do You Want?

Advertisers take many approaches to peddling their wares, but the financial services industry is odd in that it takes a very narrow focus in its approach. Most major financial providers in their ads highlight two to three areas: It's either

- How well they've done in the past
- The reams of technology they have that are going to allow you to get ahead of the other guy, or
- The efficient customer service

Of the three, the third is an obvious selling point used by most businesses, which leaves the two that are unique to financial services. The first point is useless—past performance is, of course, meaningless—and the second is nothing special in an age when the lay investor can get their hands on a pretty good program to chart their investments through their individual bank account.

ING Direct is notable, however, for its unique approach. You've probably seen these ads, where individuals walk around the city with a gigantic number under their arm, usually in the range of $1 million to $2 million. This, they say, is "Your Number," and it's the expected amount of money you'll need to have when you retire based on what you want to live on and the savings you have now. There's one commercial that's particularly memorable, where a man carrying his number (approximately $1 million or so) stops to talk to his neighbor trimming his hedges, and explains the figure he needs helps him set goals for savings and investment. He notices his neighbor's number which is "A Gazillion," and he says, "A gazillion, huh?" The poor slob cutting his bushes says, "Yeah, a gazillion...billion." He's asked how he plans for that, and he says, "I just throw a lot of money at it and hope something good happens!" His more enlightened neighbor says, "So you don't really have a plan?" He responds, sheepishly, "I have no plan..." before clamming up, and returning to the hedges.

It's mind-boggling that nobody else has stolen this idea. After all, financial companies are world-class thieves when it comes to ripping off the other guy's idea, whether it's a new structured product (like all of those debt products that nearly bankrupted the economy), mutual fund, or type of technology. But determining how much you need to retire on to have a comfortable yearly income is about as important as it gets—it focuses you on understanding how much risk you have to take in your portfolio, whether you're saving enough, and whether you're spending too much. Obviously nothing is certain in this life, particularly in the future, and as life interferes as it tends to do, your allocations may need to change, or you may need to risk more to improve your returns, or perhaps risk less because you've got enough socked away to live on for later.

But without an idea of what you plan on living on when you retire (particularly because you can probably expect to live another 20 or 30 years after you stop working), you've got no road map. Therefore, the first item on the checklist is to figure this out—and the basic rule of thumb is that you'll need about 75 percent of your income, but that bar should probably be set a little higher if you're 20 or 30 years away from retirement as your income will increase over time and inflation will mean your current 75 percent isn't going to be enough. So start with that, considering your yearly expenses through figuring out a budget, and then you'll be able to see just how much you need through your retirement contributions and the design of your retirement plan.

There are a number of providers—and many who have a 401(k) plan can take advantage of this—that can look at your investments and determine, based on conservative expectations, how close you are to reaching your goals. They use something known as Monte Carlo simulations, a process that goes through millions of scenarios to figure out what you're most likely to end up with (and usually it'll tell you what your low-end scenario is if things don't work out well). You can even input your credit card bills, worth of your house, and other expenses. The best approach here is to be as conservative as possible, building in the worst-case scenario whenever you can—figure on retirement at a relatively early age, such as 63 or 64, rather than later, because if you plan for an earlier end of work you'll have more saved even if you work longer. And assume you'll need more, not less—if you go out and figure you need one-third of your current income you'll fall short!

Then, it's time to get to the portfolios. Often brokerages or financial advisors suggest investors look at how much risk they want to take and how much they're willing to lose, and as David Loeper of Financeware puts it, "design a portfolio that's designed to lose exactly that much." That's not really the way to go—it's more important to understand how much you need and how you're going to achieve it. And if you can get to this goal by age 65 (assuming that's a retirement age and not 62 when you're first eligible) with minimal risk, so be it. If not, you have to consider more aggressive investing.

So that's first on the list. After that, it's time to take care of as much of your debt as possible. Credit card debts should be consolidated, or shifted to credit cards that can give you temporary interest rate breaks, or perhaps to some kind of home equity loan that you can pay back at a lower interest rate than the credit cards. The credit card companies are insidious—one missed payment and your rates get jacked up, and closing accounts because of this may be fine but can also dent your credit score. For the most part, you want those cards to be paid off because you're giving up a higher interest rate every year than you can earn back from the stock market. It should be noted that the same is not the case for a mortgage. A 30-year fixed rate mortgage on average is about 6 percent right now. Your investments may not get you that much, but if the home steadily appreciates in value, it will at least keep up with inflation and perhaps more, so this debt is a bit more manageable and makes sense. The same goes, somewhat less so, for an auto loan. If you can get financing at a very low rate, you're in position to save money elsewhere and pay that debt. (If you have zero percent financing, well, that's as good as a loan from your grandfather, and makes sense to take advantage of that.) If you're going to be paying an exorbitant rate, by all means take your monthly savings and add it into the car payments, and pay *that* off, too. Cars, unlike houses, are depreciating assets. They start to lose value the moment you drive them off the lot, and so it behooves you to pay as little over the original price of the car as possible.

The Portfolio

From here it's time to figure out how you're going to invest. Some asset classes are harder to source than others—such as bank loans or bank debt and certain commodities. Some are a snap. If you know what kind of risk you should be taking, it's time to divvy up the money into various different asset classes. If you have several million dollars socked away and you're 59 years old, well, it's time to stick to fixed income. Meanwhile, if you're 23 and just starting out you can afford to get as aggressive as you want because your assets are limited, and so losses incurred won't bite the way they would if you're nearing the end. (Some would argue in favor of borrowing money to invest at this age, but I'm not going to go that route.)

Your employer-sponsored retirement accounts may not have the range of choices that you want, and if not, an individual retirement account can serve as an offset to that. Having a 401(k) means you won't be able to make contributions to that account on a tax-free basis, which complicates things a little bit, but there are ways to get around this. Either way, if one account isn't going to give you the diversification you need, a second account with the freedom to buy things like commodity-focused funds or real estate or the like will help you find this diversification.

Now that we've gotten that out of the way, let's start with dividing up the portfolio into a few classes of assets. Stocks are obviously going to take up a nice percentage, with that divided into domestic, international, and emerging markets, and possibly some kind of small-cap fund, depending on the availability of total market funds. Next, there are commodities—an investment in one generalized commodity fund will do if it is low-cost. After that there are various types of debt: short-term Treasury debt, long-term Treasury debt, corporate debt, international or emerging market debt, and inflation-protected securities, which will help offset some of the drag on some investments as a result of inflation. Of course, there's always a need to have short-term cash at the ready, but that should be in your regular savings account. Since money-market funds are returning nothing at the moment, the advantage to those funds is slim other than having it as a relatively liquid source to add more to your other accounts. Putting all of that together, we find we have three primary equity classes, five types of debt, and commodities, for a total of nine. Cash, one supposes, would be counted as the tenth. There are other potential classes, including REITs, bank debt, and currencies, but the more esoteric the investment, the higher the expense ratio, and the goal here is to try to keep costs low.

So let's start with equities. It's important not to make equities too much of your portfolio, but their superior overall returns demand investment here, with a significant portion devoted to some kind of international stock index next to domestic stocks. If bonds are going to take up a bit more of the portfolio than what would normally be recommended for an aggressive investor, and commodities are going to play a role as well, then equities probably aren't going to be much more than half of your investments. What's notable about this approach, though, is that only about a quarter of the money will be geared to U.S. stocks, and even less toward the biggest U.S. stocks. Most individuals in the past have centered portfolios around large U.S. stocks, but a diversified portfolio should look elsewhere, so large U.S. stocks probably will be less than a fifth of your investments.

Look at what's available in your 401(k) plan. It's time to gravitate to anything advertised as an index fund. The expense ratios here should be very low—and the lion's share of your stock investments should be in that place. Does your 401(k) offer total market funds? You need to start there rather than an S&P 500 index fund because outperformance is often found in smaller stocks and because a portfolio that becomes more steadily weighted in favor of larger stocks runs the risk of bigger losses in the case of a downturn. Fundamentally weighted funds, those that place less emphasis on the bigger names, are an intriguing choice as well, but they form a small part of the market now. The best bet against being overly leveraged in larger stocks is a total market fund—be it one that follows the Wilshire 5000 or the Russell 3000—and probably where about a third of your equity assets should be headed. If this option isn't available, but a small-cap index fund is, then you'd need to split between a small-cap index and the rest in the large-cap index fund that's more than likely following the S&P 500. If you'd rather weight even more in favor of small stocks and a total market fund is available, buy that and a small-cap index fund, as it will shift things even further to smaller names.

The next component is the one that covers international stocks: It's preferable if your 401(k) or IRA offers the ability to buy some emerging markets stocks because those areas are primed for more growth in coming years and still offer some diversification from domestic stocks (not enough to make these two portions the mainstay, but some). It's a big world, and so you shouldn't assume you can merely put 10 or 15 percent of your assets there, but more like 35 percent of your stock investments. Now, that's not to say you'd want to dump it all into a Nigerian drilling concern (or worse, a guy on e-mail who claims to have $8 million for you if you just give up your bank account numbers), but some kind of diversified index fund will do the trick. Again, there are plenty of available ETFs that cover international stocks through an index that will keep your costs low, afford diversification in the actual market, and therefore enhance returns. Things get a bit more difficult to figure out when you get into the realm of emerging markets. Unlike regular international indexes that will still have a very low expense ratio, emerging market ETFs are sometimes a bit pricier, again, because the markets in question are at times less liquid than European, Japanese, or U.S. markets.

The popular iShares ETF that follows emerging markets has a 0.72 percent expense ratio, but Vanguard's Emerging Markets ETF has a 0.27 percent expense ratio, which actually is lower-cost than the company's similar mutual fund. The company's emerging markets mutual fund has a 0.4 percent expense ratio—unless you're investing $100,000 or more, so the ETF is getting you institutional-level pricing at a lower cost, and with tax advantages to boot. Again, there are trading costs associated with ETFs, but if your transactions are limited to just a couple per year, the erosion in returns as a result won't be terribly significant. Anyway, figure to take about half of your investment in the international space and put that in emerging markets and the rest in developed markets. If your 401(k) doesn't offer this, an IRA will be able to do so, and the 401(k) can put the funds into a diversified international fund to at least have some exposure there.

There—that's half of your money, split by thirds between domestic shares, emerging markets, and developed markets. That's a solid basis for growth and doesn't depend on any one region of the world.

With 50 percent of your portfolio taken care of, it probably makes you wonder, with a title such as *Never Buy Another Stock Again*, why am I advocating so much of your money in the equity market? Well, equities have performed more strongly than most other assets, as you well know, but the low cost associated with the investments that have been set forth here will maximize those returns as much as possible. The other classes of assets are harder to find and cost a bit more but will be an important part of your portfolio as well—and that's commodities, short-term government debt, long-term debt, and then a couple of others that may end up in the mix as well. There are those who argue that all of these asset classes should be divvied up equally, and that's possible to do as well; it requires a bigger bet on commodities, real estate, and corporate bonds. In that case, shrink the equity portion down by about 20 percent or so and shift some of that into the other categories. This makes sense as well because it adds to diversification and provides other avenues for strong performance. We'll get back to investing in bonds in a minute, but it's notable that some companies, such as Vanguard, offer low-cost ETFs in the corporate bond world; the Vanguard Long-Term Corporate Bond ETF has a 0.15 percent expense ratio, once again keeping costs at the low end.

The other source of growth in one's portfolio can belong to hard assets. Real estate ETFs are popular, as they invest in Real Estate Investment Trusts, companies set up with a focus on a certain type of real estate, be it by type of construction or location. The problem you encounter is if you're already a homeowner, you've already got massive exposure to the local real estate market through your house, and it makes the case for real estate less convincing.

The next option is commodities. Here's where things get tricky—retirement providers aren't generally offering these options as readily as they are stock and bond investments (and some venture into the world of REITs), so that's the purpose of having an IRA account that gives you the freedom to buy other things. Remember, you're going to be rebalancing based on your entire spectrum of investments, so it's important not to segregate this account for one asset, but for a couple, and so a smattering of your portfolio should be kept in equity and bonds in this account so you're able to rebalance away and to these various assets without giving yourself the headache of switching accounts. Since participation in a 401(k) means you're not allowed to contribute to an IRA tax-free, the best option for funding that account is through taking an existing one from a previous employer and effecting a rollover (or putting your initial seed money for the IRA with capital that's already been taxed, although again, that's less optimal). Now that you've got this money there, there are a number of commodity fund options, but the problem is the expenses are high. The iShares Silver Trust, which invests in silver, is one of the cheaper ones, with a 0.5 percent expense ratio, but most diversified commodity funds cost a bit more, from 0.8 percent to 0.95 percent. That's not the kind of hit you want to take in your portfolio on a yearly basis, but if the rest of your expenses can be kept low, for 10 percent of your assets, it can be tolerated.

The bond market comes next. There are a number of low-cost options that target investment-grade bonds—those are bonds sold by companies thought to have the best chance of paying that money back to the investor—such as the Vanguard entry, which sports a low 0.15 percent expense ratio. High-yield funds are a bit more money (the State Street SPDRs high-yield fund has a 0.40 percent expense ratio, while the iShares version has a 0.50 percent cost), but that's still relatively low for an investor to consider it. Another consideration would be convertible securities, which are bonds that carry stocklike characteristics. State Street offers an ETF in this area as well, and again, the expense ratio isn't terrible, at 0.4 percent of assets. There are also ways to gain exposure to international debt, but it's a bit more difficult and costlier. That doesn't mean it's not possible, however.

If 20 percent of your assets goes into various types of corporate debt, that's 80 percent. Where does the rest go? Well, another 10 percent should be in the government market, of which some of that has to be in short-term debt, which has the advantage of repricing quickly when inflation hits. Finally, there are plenty of funds that offer the option of investing in Treasury inflation protected securities (TIPs), and they're another inflation hedge. The money in the bond funds, including government bonds, should also help protect against a downturn in overall markets.

So what does this all look like when mapped out, for now (see Table 10.1)?

TABLE 10.1 Hypothetical Asset Allocation

Asset Class	Percent
Stocks	50
Commodities	10
Corporate Long-Term Debt	20
Govt. Debt/TIPS	20

Let's try to take a look at what the expenses will be like for such a portfolio. Let's assume you've got $100,000, and work from there. The following investments mentioned in Table 10.2 are not meant as recommendations, and they won't be available to everyone; they've been chosen as representative low-cost purchases.

TABLE 10.2 Hypothetical Investment Selections

Investment	Ratio	Pct	Cost
Vanguard Total Market	0.09	25	$22.50
Schwab Int'l Equity	0.15	12.5	$18.75
Vanguard Em Mkts	0.27	12.5	$33.75
DB Cmdty Svcs Fund	0.93	10	$93.00
SPDR Barclays HY Fund	0.40	10	$40.00
SPDR Long-Term Credit	0.15	10	$15.00
SPDR Barclays T-Bill ETF	0.1345	7	$9.40
SPDR Bclys Lg-Tm Treas	0.1345	7	$9.40
SPDR TIPS ETF	0.1845	6	$11.07

Adding that all up brings the total annual cost to $252.87, or an annual expense ratio of a very manageable 0.253 percent of your assets. It would be difficult to go much cheaper than this unless you elect to stick to long-term credit or corporate debt without bothering with high-yield debt, and if you eliminate commodities altogether. This, of course, does not factor in trading costs. A discount broker-age's trading cost of about $10 per trade—and assuming a once-a-year rebalancing that necessitates buys and sales of a percentage of all of these funds—adds another $100 to the cost, still putting your costs around 0.35 percent of your assets, which is not a lot. Do you think it's too much? Go look at your current portfolio and see if you're already spending more and if there are no shorter-term options. In addition, if you consider that some of these investments (and hopefully most of them) are being held in mutual funds rather than ETFs you may be able to escape some of the costs associated with the ETFs. Once again, you still have to consider the costs of buying ETFs periodically since only Schwab and Fidelity (using iShares ETFs) are offering commission-free buying of ETFs, which is again part of why you'd have to find a workaround. Either you fund an IRA once with a rollover from a previous employer, or you set aside contributions that wouldn't be made to the 401(k) plan and use that to fund the IRA. But there are prohibitions on rollovers from a plan where you're employed, which makes it more difficult.

The Risk Factor

Does the plan listed above look too risky? Well, it's notable that a number of the asset classes you're now holding, including emerging markets stocks, commodities, long-dated Treasuries, TIPs, short-term debt, and high-yield debt, were all better than U.S. large-cap stocks, which have been the mainstay of investment portfolios for years. In fact, if you've divided your U.S. stock investment equally between a large-cap index and one that follows a small-cap index, it means just 12.5 percent of your portfolio is in the big U.S. titans. You've got plenty of exposure to stocks, but you're not overdoing it in the category that hasn't done much for investors for the better part of ten years now. But, you say, what if they come back? Well, they might—and they might outdo all comers. But if large-company stocks in the U.S. are going to do well in the next decade, small companies are going to do well, too. If large-company U.S. stocks are going to rock the world from now until 2020, well, many of them operate worldwide, so stocks outside the U.S. will be in good shape as well, and the same goes for international stocks. But the portfolio outlined above also has a measure of protection against inflation, it has enough debt to keep something moving in the right direction if the stock market languishes, and it has exposure to assets that should not be correlated with anything else.

If you're a more conservative investor, you're more likely to want to keep things a bit closer to the vest, and that may mean including more bonds in the portfolio, and a reduction in equity assets. But here's another area where investors may need to change a bit—unless you're so averse to losing any money, ever, your future needs are going to have to determine the risk you're going to take. If you are unable to achieve the retirement you like without working until you're 80 on a steady diet of Treasury bonds and certificates of deposit, you're going to have to get more aggressive, and that means getting more comfortable with taking on a portfolio that will be more volatile but offer the prospect of better returns. The other choice is to live more frugally, socking away more of your current income, and then you could tilt toward the more conservative end of the spectrum. You're more likely to be able to be conservative later in life if you're more open to risk earlier on, but also if you're putting money away. At age 62, the only benefit you're going to get from the savings you're putting away is just that—the savings—as the compounding that comes from having money in the bank for years will only have a few years to grow. Some of what will help determine your investment will be, once again, figuring out your needs.

The one other determinant is, of course, how the markets handle the next few decades. Even though this has been a tumultuous period, it does not necessarily follow that a rough-and-tumble decade paves the way for a benign, relatively boring one where markets go up unimpeded in the way they did in the 1990s. The more likely development is that markets will be a bit more uneasy due to the great imbalances that exist as a result of profligate spending by governments in the 2000s and the overextended credit profile of America's consumers. David Rosenberg, chief market strategist at Gluskin Sheff in Toronto and a longtime market follower, noted in commentary that the post-crash period was not one that was immediately restored to a steady, unyielding growth path, but instead the 1930s to 1954 was "a multi-year tumultuous period that was racked by volatility and manic market performance," and the most successful move was to try to "immunize the portfolio from the massive ups-and-downs." As this book comes to a close, it's worthwhile to look at the bigger picture going forward, how things stand, and what investors are worried about in the coming years.

Boiling It Down

- Enforcing a savings discipline is key to building a nest egg. You eventually adjust to not spending that small amount of money you're putting away. Have your bank automatically transfer $20 (at least) into your savings account per week.
- Don't run up your credit card debt; pay off those debts that you can or at least consolidate debts to a card with a better interest rate.
- Keep your costs low—listen to John Bogle. Your largest portfolio holdings should be the lowest-cost ones.

- Diversifying does not simply refer to stocks. It is possible to own several different stock classes, as well as several types of bonds, such as corporate bonds, high-yield and municipal, as well as agency and government securities, at a relatively low cost.

- Rebalance your portfolio, but be sure to do it with as few trades as possible.

- Take advantage of company matches in 401(k) or other retirement plans.

- Use stop loss orders to save yourself from extreme market declines and stick to limit orders to get the price you want when selling or buying.

- How much money do you need to retire on? Figure out that number and work towards it. Be prepared to adjust your goals if your investments do not perform up to snuff for a number of years, and that means saving more, investing in riskier assets with a chance of better returns, or retiring later in life.

Endnote

[1] Adam Y. C. Lei and Huihua Li, "The Value of Stop-Loss Strategies," *Financial Services Review* 18 (2009), 23-51.

11

The Outlook for the Future

"The last ten years have produced very bad returns...but you talk to people and they still think equities are wonderful. I don't dispute it—I think equities are a good long-term investment. What worries me in the short-run is how unanimous that vision is."

Andrew Smithers, president, Smithers & Co., London, January 2010

To invest in the success of Corporate America over the past 35 years, investors would have done well by buying and holding an S&P 500 index fund. Warren Buffett said as much in his 2004 letter to clients.

But that simple strategy may not be the winning formula for the next 35 years. There are legitimate concerns about what the next generation of growth will look like for U.S. markets and markets around the globe. Massive imbalances brought on by large debt issuance have created problems for several large societies, but most notably the U.S. and Japan, which in 2010 were still the two largest economies in the world. It is, therefore, legitimate to ask whether the U.S. will be the equivalent of a "growth stock" in the next few decades, or whether it is a busted growth stock—something that retains a high value largely on reputation despite mediocre economic demand for a number of years.

For a look at what may happen in the next several years, let's look at the 1966 to 1982 period, a time that was also marked by lackluster economic activity. Wage growth was reasonably strong, but rising inflation and a crushing bubble in energy prices eroded a lot of those gains. The U.S. was taken off the gold standard while inflation leaked into the economy due to a series of poor decisions by ineffectual Federal Reserve chairmen.

This 1966-1982 period was a great one in the market if an investor knew when to hold 'em and when to fold 'em, as Kenny Rogers would say. Stocks experienced a handful of sharp rallies in this period of time, offset by a number of ugly downturns. For the index investor, it was a rough period, with the S&P and Dow in 1982 roughly in the same place as in 1966. Between January 1966 and August 1982, when the market turned definitively higher, there were four big, solid bull markets, five ugly bear markets, and one lackluster trading range that lasted about two years (see Table 11.1).

TABLE 11.1   Bull and Bear Markets, 1966 to 1982

Bear/Bull	Dates	Returns
Bear	Jan. 66-Oct. 66	-25.1
Bull	Oct. 66-Nov. 68	+32.4%
Bear	Nov. 68-May 70	-35.9%
Bull	May 70-Jan. 73	+66.6%
Bear	Jan. 73-Dec. 74	-45.1%
Bull	Dec. 74-Sept. 76	+75%
Bear	Sept. 76-Mar. 78	-26.8%
Bull	Mar. 78-Apr. 80	+2.2%
Bull	Apr. 80-Apr. 81	+37.9%
Bear	Apr. 81-Aug. 82	-24.1%

Looking at this roller coaster 16 years, there are clear time periods investors should have avoided, and several periods investors would have laughed all the way to the bank. These took place amid long recessions, the energy crisis of the late 1970s, and America's worst bout of inflation in more than a century.

The last decade, 2000-2010, has been similar, although the runs have been a bit less frequent. Stocks were terrible between the 2000 peak and the trough reached in mid-2003, but then went on a relatively steady four-year run that took shares to new records in late 2007. After that, it's been a roller coaster more easily identified with the 1970s, as shares lost half of their value between October 2007 and March 2009, when the S&P 500 hit a 12-year-low, and then gained back more than 70 percent through the end of March 2010. Many a smart investor missed a good lot of that period—the Investment Company Institute shows net outflows from domestic equity funds in every month from August 2009 to December 2009. Meanwhile, if you stuck it out with a buy-and-hold strategy for the bulk of the decade, you're still underwater with a diminished time horizon to make up for those losses.

Expectations in coming years suggest a need to be nimble. The massive unwind of debt on corporate balance sheets and the time it will take for the restoration of growth engines in the U.S. economy mean that the market will experience several more "boom-and-bust" episodes. The stock market will be a wild, unpredictable place as a result.

For those who suggest that this cycle—the period of stagnating in returns—is bound to come to a close soon anyway because the market has already experienced nine flat years, should reconsider that optimistic view. If the market does follow a similar cycle as last time, then the next long bull run should commence late in the decade after a few more years of stagnation. Again, for a 12-year-old, this is fine, but for those rapidly closing in on retirement, or currently in the midst of their best years for investing, waiting it out isn't a sound idea. After the stock market peaked in 1929, it underwent a 25-year period of flat markets before it started to trend higher in the mid-1950s. And the sharp gains prior to this only lasted for a short period of time, from about 1921 to 1929—before that, the market endured about 21 years of Nowheresville as well.

While stocks may have seemed cheap in February 2009, the 60 percent rally meant stocks weren't all that cheap anymore, according to Research Affiliates Inc. With stocks at a price-to-earnings ratio of 20 to 22 times trailing 12-month earnings, they were at levels that, when reached in the past, generally translated to lackluster returns for a period of years. Table 11.2 outlines what happened in the ten-year periods after stocks reached such P/E ratios.

TABLE 11.2   High P/E Ratios Don't Translate to Strong Markets

Years	10-yr Returns	Inflation
1928-1930	-1.6%	-1.9%
1936-1937	+6.1%	+6.3%
1960s	+6.3%	+4.7%
1992-1995	+10.6%	+2.4%

Source: Research Affiliates[1]

Of the four periods, the ten-year period after the mid-1990s was obviously an exception. The first one is the Depression, while the second two produce decent returns that are eaten up by higher than usual inflation. It's hard right now to fathom another Depression, although the economic recovery in mid-2010 has been flagging. We're more likely to see an overheat in asset prices than some kind of collapse as a result of too-little support for the markets. It's true that after a brief rebound in late 2009 and early 2010, pundits are calling for austerity measures out of the U.S. government, but if the economy slips again, more stimulus will be applied to "shock" the economy out of its stupor.

Can investors handle another decade of this? It isn't a strong value proposition for investors who aren't engaged in altering their asset allocation in coming years. In the first place, if your investing horizon is less than 70 years, "you can't count on the long-term average of the market because you're not going to be in it long enough to see how it turns out," said Ken Kam of Marketocracy, which tracks investors' portfolios on its Web site.

As 2009 came to a close, investors were feeling optimistic. A buoyant set of economic reports suggested the environment was on the mend, but a number of factors suggest growth will be lower in coming years than it had been in the late 1990s and mid-2000s. Many don't want to be confronted with the reality that investment returns just aren't going to be what people got used to—not if they're sticking exclusively to U.S. big-cap stocks, anyway—and assume that everything that dies will someday come back. That's a bad assumption.

Debt is the foremost factor that will block investors from earning the same kind of returns as they did through the 1990s. The U.S. owes a lot of people a lot of money, and much of the income generated by investors, companies, and government institutions will be spent servicing that debt rather than paying for new research and development or improved infrastructure. Of course, the U.S. is not an impoverished nation, like so many in Africa that are struggling to provide services to their citizens because of massive debts incurred by dictators in the past. Nor is it Argentina, which underwent a series of crises as a result of its heavy debt burden.

But the U.S., as of the end of 2009, had a debt level that fell short of just a few other countries in the world. In terms of debt levels as a percentage of our gross domestic product, we're doing all right— ranked about 66th in the world in 2009, with debt amounting to about 39.7 percent of our total GDP, according to the CIA's yearly World Factbook. (By far the worst-off is Zimbabwe, which has debt obligations of about 300 percent of GDP.)

That doesn't tell the whole story, though. Our current account balance, which is a measure of our trade in goods, services, interest payments and profits, and a few other things, is at a negative $706 billion. That ranks worst in the world, and the second-worst, Spain, is nowhere near us, with a current account deficit of $154 billion.

When state and local governments are included, public debt continues to rise. Adding in household and corporate debt pushes the U.S.'s debt-to-GDP ratio to about 840 percent of GDP, which is plainly unsustainable. The Federal Reserve took on a big load of these obligations, in effect transferring them from corporate balance sheets to the federal government's balance sheet. "Growth in the U.S. is going to be hampered by our debt burden for years to come," said Rob Arnott, founder of Research Associates. "We are so addicted to debt that our debt burden is quite literally beyond anything any nation in world history has ever achieved."

A McKinsey study pegs the U.S. debt as a percentage of GDP at 300 percent—which still trails the U.K. at 466 percent and Japan at 471 percent. And John Mauldin, chief investment officer at Millennium Wave Investments in Fort Worth, Texas, said in a recent commentary that deleveraging has a long way to go in the United States—perhaps another five or six years before the leverage accumulated over a period of decades is reduced to a more manageable level.

Other countries are more hampered by their debt levels, and concern about the financial health of those nations helped U.S. markets in late 2009 and early 2010 as the U.S. came to be regarded as the "best kid in the bad neighborhood." U.S. Treasury debt remained at low yields, and that market continued to see substantial appetite for frequent sales of government securities as foreigners bought our long-term debt in lieu of purchases in troubled areas such as the euro zone, where the rising fiscal imbalances in the likes of Greece, Spain, and Portugal threatened to undermine the euro and other markets in that region.

But being the best-looking pile of garbage in the garbage dump isn't anything to be proud of. The U.S. faces mostly unsatisfactory choices: raising taxes, reducing government spending, or, worst of all, default. The latter isn't any kind of choice at all. Russia and Argentina both defaulted on debt, in 1998 and 2001, respectively, and a country that defaults quickly finds itself without a lot of friends in the investing world. Interest rates would likely soar, borrowing costs would become cost-prohibitive, and the dollar would get hit even worse than it has already been beaten up in recent years; it would be a disaster for the public debt and corporations alike.

What is more likely is that the U.S. continues in the current vein—a period of deleveraging, where companies try to pay down debt, while the government sector takes on more leverage to ward off depression-type conditions. At this point, in 2010, the economy appears to have escaped a depression, but the recession has been a devastating one, with double-digit unemployment, and the weight of government deficits and the poor decisions made by the private sector for several years are likely to result in an economy that grows more slowly for several years, if not more. Part of this is the consequence of profligate actions by the government during the first decade of this century, and unfortunately, while some may believe deficits can be ignored, they cannot—all bills have to be paid eventually. This, Pacific Asset Management's Bill Gross argues, will hurt returns in coming years in the U.S., along with several other large industrialized nations.

The current political climate has only a small appetite for a robust Keynesian response. This refers to economist John Maynard Keynes, the Depression-era advocate of pump-priming government spending to shock an economy out of a severe depression. So in early 2010 Barack Obama, the U.S. president, started to talk of deficit reduction through targeted spending freezes. This was not meant to apply to certain entitlements, but the public's strange desire to see the government's balance sheet repaired to the extent that individuals and corporations have not repaired themselves is a bit misplaced, particularly decisions made in the middle of 2010 to cut off extensions of unemployment benefits, which will only hurt the economy more. It is, however, the reality of the United States, and such an effort also means that social programs will be taking a back seat to other efforts.

What this may do, unfortunately, is open up the possibility that the U.S. economy will backslide in terms of growth, after a surge that took the U.S. out of recession in late 2009/early 2010, at least temporarily. Double-dip recessions are rare indeed—the last one experienced in the U.S. took place amid an energy crisis and a massive rise in interest rates between 1980 and 1982. The U.S. entered recession in January 1980, was out by July 1980, and slipped back in just 12 months later, according to the National Bureau of Economic Research, responsible for determining the cycle of business expansions and contractions. The last instance where two recessions followed so closely was in the aftermath of World War I. Many economists believe the extensive stimulus undertaken, along with policy efforts by the Federal Reserve, will keep the economy out of the abyss. But final demand remains weak, industrial activity is slack, and hiring is anemic, all recipes for a sluggish economic environment, and one that does not justify the 70 percent rally in stocks between March 2009 and March 2010.

So it's back to the see-saw approach, one that wreaks havoc on those who elect to sit back and invest passively in index funds and not check their situation at the end of each month or at worst, at the end of the quarter. As the spring of 2010 wore on, economic data suggested a reasonable improvement in demand, but many investors, including Doug Kass, president of Seabreeze Partners Management in Palm Beach, Florida, said the rebound reflected an ongoing snapback from the period of late 2008 and early 2009 when consumers were more or less catatonic. As government stimulus programs wane, the possibility of subpar growth looms. Subpar does not refer to endless recessions—but 1 percent to 2 percent annual growth in gross domestic product, which is slow enough that stocks and other investment assets are likely to bounce to and fro, even after the massive 70 percent rally that the market has just experienced.

"I think you're going to see the boom-and-bust cycle continue," says Michael Lewitt, who heads the hedge fund Harch Capital

Management in Boca Raton, Florida. "I see real issues in terms of trying to figure out what to do about the deficit, and I think it's going to be a very, very difficult environment to make significant money in. You're going to have to be willing to go short to really outperform. I don't see the market itself growing tremendously—I see a lot of money that's going to have to be diverted to servicing debt at the federal and state level."[2]

Professors Ken Rogoff of Harvard and Carmen Reinhart of the University of Maryland have catalogued the average declines in the aftermath of full-scale banking crises like those that occurred in the U.S. They note that real housing price declines average about 35 percent over a six-year period, and equity prices fall by about 55 percent.[3] Employment and output continue to suffer, and government debt rises to unheard of levels, largely because of the collapse in tax revenues as a result of the crisis. That's where the economy is now. It's a dire outlook for sure, and Rogoff/Reinhart have found that unemployment levels tend to remain elevated for five years after they rise sharply, putting the U.S. on track for a substantial rebound in job growth somewhere around 2015. Notably, unemployment in the late spring of 2010 was still close to 10 percent, and a broader measure of unemployment that factors in those who have ceased to look for a job was in the high teens. Such a job market does not argue well for continued investment gains, even if the wealthiest of consumers continued to spend. While some economic indicators suggest an improvement, the National Federation of Independent Businesses, which tracks the activity of small businesses nationwide, issued a dire outlook in April 2010, noting that small firm capital spending was at a 35-year-low and plans for future expenditures also remained low.[4]

An optimistic sort would respond to this sluggish commentary by suggesting that since equities and real estate have already suffered their requisite downturn, the markets should be on the verge of recovery. That is indeed possible—and part of the reason why many strategists have moved back into equities, particularly as the rally of

2009 got underway. But with a 70 percent rebound in stocks having already taken place, the best opportunity may already be past, especially as the economy continues to unwind from years of excessive leverage, and as valuation already suggests investors are pricing a lot of growth into an economy that may not deliver on lofty expectations.

Plenty of investors continue to prefer equities. But the reality is that see-sawing markets are likely to be the dominant condition for the next decade, especially if structural problems, such as the lack of effective regulation of financial institutions, are not addressed. The idea of another decade of flat returns is unacceptable, which is why smart investors believe the buy-and-hold approach has been consigned to the dustbin of history.

What appears to be the reality here is that the uncertain growth path of the U.S. and other developed nations in coming years due to rising debt levels will make allocating effectively, particularly to emerging markets, more important. It means they will also have to invest in corporate debt of well-run companies, as that can provide strong returns as companies have to continue to service their debts.

The Inflation Question

Investors are currently worried about inflation. There is some justification for this. The U.S. Federal Reserve, in concert with other world monetary authorities, is in the midst of a concerted effort to restore economic health and remove barriers to lending and capital formation in the largest global economies. With interest rates at rock-bottom levels in most major world markets, those institutions that have ready access to capital—for now that means large conglomerates—should have the means to borrow more easily to finance spending and investment.

If prices rise in the U.S. at a faster rate than our creditors, it will make our debt burden less onerous and easy to pay off, as the debts, valued in current dollars, will be easier to manage if the value of our dollars rises.

Unfortunately—and here's where this matters for the individual investor—inflationary environments are unpredictable at best and often produce middling returns.

Investors are concerned that the rapid expansion of the money supply will fuel another asset bubble, this one sponsored by the leverage undertaken by the government, rather than the private or household sectors as was the case in the previous bubbles. If asset price inflation is followed by a jump up in price inflation in the real economy, it will make the investment environment more difficult. There are a few investments that are designed to shield investment portfolios from inflation, but stocks have not always been the best choice.

"People no longer think of stocks as an inflation hedge, and based on experience, that's a reasonable conclusion for them to have reached," said Richard Cohn, an associate professor of finance at the University of Illinois, in *Business Week*'s noted "The Death of Equities" cover story. But the experience at the time was important in understanding how equities performed in light of rising inflation. *BW* quoted Salomon Brothers, which pointed out that stocks boasted a 3.1 percent compound annual rate of return between 1968 and 1979, while the consumer price index rose by 6.5 percent annually. They noted that gold, diamonds (which almost nobody considers a viable investment vehicle), and single-family housing all outpaced the stock market during that period—and the price of oil didn't do too badly, either.

One asset that certainly also runs into trouble during a period of heavy inflation is long-term bonds, particularly government bonds. With corporate debt, there's always the chance of price appreciation based on fundamental factors related to a company, but government debt is unlikely to respond in the same way. Why is this so problematic for the average person? Because you're likely to have made bonds and stocks the mainstay of your portfolio, and both assets are not in favorable positions as the next decade wears on.

Inflation has remained low for a number of years, but that trend may be ending, and certainly one of the markets that was broadly supported by falling inflation, bonds, could also have hit a peak. "You cannot make the argument now that we're on a wave of declining interest rates," says Kevin Flynn, a money manager with Avalon Asset Management. "You can argue as to whether we're going into deflation or inflation, but we're not going into a 20-year wave of falling inflation."

Certain assets have done better than others when inflation got out of control. Treasury inflation-protected securities (TIPs) are one natural way of hedging against rising inflation, but small-cap stocks, commodities, and real estate investment trusts have also been effective against inflation because they represent asset classes where prices are being constantly adjusted in recognition of a changing price environment. Small-cap stocks reflect companies that can see quick increases in their earning power as a result of rising prices, while commodities and real estate prices change in line with overall price changes in the economy (and sometimes faster). Long-term bonds, by contrast, have a set value for 10 or 30 years, and will not do well against inflation. Between January 1977 and April 1980, the inflation rate rose from about 5 percent to 14 percent on an annualized basis, and very few assets can keep up with that. A few do, however—and investors have to be ready for such a move, although probably not that drastic, in the coming years as the economy finally stabilizes.

Either way, the market could experience several more years of middling or up-and-down action. This means the buy-and-hold investor could end up holding stocks through a long slog before finally getting out, once again, selling at the wrong time. If investors end up at the same level they were ten years earlier, this puts even more pressure on that individual to outperform the averages as retirement approaches. Now a decade closer to retirement, their nest egg now relies more on the performance of investments and less on asset accumulation.

Debt Goes Around the World

The markets, as a result of the ongoing debt crises around the world, are likely to remain volatile and subject to gyrations as a result of tremors occurring in smaller countries due to the interconnectedness of financial institutions around the world. In late 2009 Dubai World, the state-controlled company based in the United Arab Emirates, said it was looking to delay its debt payments, raising fears of default by Dubai and sparking a sell-off in risk assets around the world. The emirate is still in the midst of sorting out the off- and on-balance sheet exposures to certain debts that they are struggling with as they now have to deleverage, that is, write down or pay off these debts as economic growth cannot sustain them. "Let Dubai be a reminder to all: Last year's financial crisis was a consequential phenomenon whose lagged impact is yet to play out fully in the economic, financial, institutional and political arenas," wrote Mohamed El-Erian of Pacific Investment Management in November of 2009.[5]

Stocks and bonds eventually recovered, but in early 2010, just a few months later, the markets grappled with scares of defaults out of Greece, one of the sicker countries in Europe in terms of financial health. With Greece having substantial holdings in Eastern European nations, the news hit those markets as well. Not long after that, China said it would try to restrict lending from its banks, once again damaging stocks. And then a crisis hit Portugal, as the Iberian nation found itself unable to sell as many of its own government securities as it wanted to, causing markets to gyrate once again. Spain followed. We're not close to being finished.

The commonality here is that many of these nations, during boom times, borrowed money from creditors outside the country and used it to finance various large projects, both private or public. Investors were happy as long as debt was being serviced, but shocks rippling through markets in 2008 and 2009 caused certain countries' currencies to decline in value, making debt service more difficult. As the problems individual banks had became more well-known, this resulted in a flight of capital, which only exacerbated the decline in the currency. Suddenly, loans that were easily serviced were now breaking the back of the balance sheets of banks anywhere from Iceland to Dubai. The need for nations to undergo severe restructuring programs—which will involve fewer public services and reduced economic assistance— means demand will be sluggish in a number of countries until the process of deleveraging is finished. Because of the extent of the borrowing through most of the 2000s, this is not going to be an easy time and makes it more likely that sudden eruptions in confidence will knock markets for a loop for a period of weeks or months.

This does not mean that every nation should automatically be considered suspect in terms of its debt and/or credit rating. But it does mean that investors are likely to be fickle, shifting allocations from one country to the next with wild abandon when trouble erupts. For now, Europe is the troubled area of the world, particularly the Mediterranean nations of Spain, Portugal, Greece, and Italy, along with Ireland. Eastern Europe is no picnic either. For those looking to invest internationally, diversification and more importantly, owning the entire market becomes paramount. While most indexes were hit hard in the aftershocks of 2008 and 2009, broader market indexes, such as the exchange-traded funds that followed emerging markets in general or the Europe/Asia/Far East areas were better situated than country-specific funds.

With the focus on international indexes much more intense than before, investors will have to reckon with the possibility that the U.S. will not be the world's primary growth engine anymore. This economy is still huge, but the horrid meltdown of 2008 remains fresh enough in the minds of buyers. "It used to be that if you knew domestic equities and you knew them well you were fine, and you could succeed in the game, but now it's gone international," said Chris Johnson, head of Johnson Research Group in Cincinnati, Ohio. "Look at what happened with Dubai—that's a relatively small amount of cash when you look at it. It's a drop in the bucket compared to the amount we're talking about here over the last two years, but it was able to send a pretty good ripple through the market."

With many countries facing unsustainable budget deficits, and with growth uncertain in many of the nations that have driven world economic demand in recent years, you're going to be dealing with choppy, uncertain markets for some time. It would be nice to be able to sit back, sock away the money in index funds, and forget about it, but the climate demands you pay attention. That doesn't mean making this into agony—it needn't be wrenching to try to figure out how to handle your portfolio—but above all, it will require flexibility and shedding yourself of the dogmatic approach and the clichés that pass for actual investment advice. This may mean a more active involvement in shifting assets, but those paths have their own peril, as it involves making bets at optimum moments, and many investors have a hard time doing this. It may be that it relies on tactical shifts in and out of risk assets all at once—again, a difficult chore, but one that can possibly be done with the right amount of homework. At the very least, rebalancing will limit overexposure to any one investment that has outperformed, and leave you less vulnerable to big declines in those assets.

Going Forward

This book is not meant to be a comprehensive approach to investing. It's a big world, there are a lot of investments, and plenty of smart people out there who have kept a clear head in their years as investors and managed to do well over a long period of time without things getting complicated. Really, financial security is feeling secure in your decisions today and the long-term path you're taking for years down the road.

This advice I've put forth admittedly falls into what my elders would have just called common sense. But they didn't manage to find a way to live off modest salaries for a long retirement through luck—it involved counting pennies (and rolling those pennies into rolls and depositing them into the bank) and keeping an eye out on what lay ahead. The Depression-era generation got by with their savings, guaranteed pension benefits, and social security payments—and their retirement was often just a handful of years after a lifetime of work. It is more difficult for the boomer generation. Pensions aren't what they were, subsequent generations face the possibility of reduced social security benefits, and they must take more direct involvement in their own retirement. Many of you have been scared out of your wits by this meltdown. There is time to recover—it just can't be done the same way. And it certainly can't be done by simply forgetting about it and assuming everything will work out.

This approach is not the only one, of course. But the common sense that I'm imparting shouldn't be overlooked. Most of all, keeping a clear head when it comes to your money is of prime importance. You are allowed to sell things if it will preserve assets that you don't want to lose. You can avoid buying faddish stocks or letting your investments run wild, and you still can have success that will prepare you for retirement. And once you make those decisions, don't look back on them.

I hope this book has been edifying, thought-provoking, and a bit entertaining as well. If sure answers existed in investing, people would follow the same rules, time and again, but they don't. People will continue to try to find alternate ways to build models to come out ahead of everyone else, or so they think. The investing world is going to be an increasingly complex, volatile one. It doesn't have to be a crazy experience for you, though. Simple rules can help preserve your money—and your sanity.

Boiling It Down

- Be prepared for anything in the next ten years. The stock market could go nowhere; it isn't destined to rise just because it has been suffering for most of a decade.

- Look to allocate assets in areas where debt is not the overriding factor, such as in many emerging markets. For another twist on that, well-managed companies with limited amounts of debt are potential bond market investments (through an index of high-rated corporate bonds).

- Common sense rules. Save your pennies and invest them in the markets carefully, keeping your costs low and your trading minimal.

- Avoid fads like the plague. If everyone is doing it, eventually it's not going to feel good for anyone.

- Index funds and exchange-traded funds that mimic indexes are great building blocks for a well-managed, low-cost portfolio.

- Don't forget about rebalancing.

- Expect see-sawing markets to continue. Make sure you don't have more than about a quarter of your assets in large-cap domestic stocks; investing in commodities, various types of bonds, and emerging markets should help offset the volatile stock market.

- Avoid following advice based on clichés or aphorisms.

- Don't be afraid to sell a losing asset.

- Admit it—you don't know everything. And that's okay.

Endnotes

[1]"Fundamentals: Lessons from the 'Naughties,'" Research Affiliates, February 2010.

[2]Author interview.

[3]Carmen M. Reinhart and Kenneth S. Rogoff, "The Aftermath of Financial Crises," December 19, 2008, paper prepared for American Economic Association meetings in San Francisco, California, January 3, 2009.

[4]NFIB Small Business Economic Trends, April 2010, http://www.nfib.com/Portals/0/PDF/sbet/SBET201004.pdf.

[5]Mohamed El-Erian, "Dubai: What the Immediate Future Holds," *The Daily Telegraph*, November 29, 2009, http://www.telegraph.co.uk/finance/economics/6678194/Dubai-what-the-immediate-future-holds.html.

Bibliography

Works Frequently Cited:

Stocks for the Long Run: The Definitive Guide to Financial Market Returns and Long Term Investment Strategies, Jeremy J. Seigel, McGraw-Hill Companies

The Little Book of Common Sense Investing: The Only Way to Guarantee Your Fair Share of Stock Market Returns, by John C. Bogle, 2007, Wiley Publishing

Jim Cramer's Real Money: Sane Investing in an Insane World, Simon & Schuster, 2009

Triumph of the Optimists: 101 Years of Global Investment Returns, Elroy Dimson, Paul Marsh, and Mike Staunton, Princeton University Press, 2002

INDEX

FINANCIAL TIMES

In an increasingly competitive world, it is quality
of thinking that gives an edge—an idea that opens new
doors, a technique that solves a problem, or an insight
that simply helps make sense of it all.

We work with leading authors in the various arenas
of business and finance to bring cutting-edge thinking
and best-learning practices to a global market.

It is our goal to create world-class print publications
and electronic products that give readers
knowledge and understanding that can then be
applied, whether studying or at work.

To find out more about our business
products, you can visit us at www.ftpress.com.